Simon's a poof's name.

1. No Breakfast.

2. "Spike! I like Spike".

3. HMS Plymouth.

4. New Romantics.

5. At Sea.

6. Bunting Tosser.

7. Big D.

8. Slog (the daily grind).

9. The Russian Submarine Incident.

10. Windies Deployment.

11. 2nd April 1982.

12. "Beam Me Up Scotty".

13. Little Bit From Knotty.

14. Since '82.

SIMON'S A POOF'S NAME.

No Breakfast

I looked at the 'draft list' that was pinned to the noticeboard. It was a list informing everyone of which ship they'd been drafted to after the end of our training as Radio Operators at HMS Mercury.

Mercury was a shore base in East Meon, near Petersfield, Hants, it is now a housing estate I believe. There was a big old house where the Captain lived, that had a parade ground in front of it, a place where we spent hours perfecting the art of standing still for ages and being shouted at. Other skills we learned were; stifling laughing and feigning fainting, or of course just plain fainting if you'd had a skinfull the night before. If you'd been unable to face breakfast or just been too late for breakfast and had to rush to get into uniform and just made parade in time, you could be in trouble. In other words you were prime for falling flat on your face! Either way you were in trouble because fainting or injuring yourself would be a 'self-inflicted injury' and your own fault for drinking too much and not eating breakfast.

Standing to attention for long periods of time, combined with one of these scenarios wasn't good. The real trick is to make sure that you are aware that you're going down and squat on one knee, rather than taking a nose dive! I feigned it once on parade, only once. We'd been stood there for ages, a freezing morning, being balled at. I just thought "fuck it, I've had enough", I wobbled a bit and went down on one knee, then someone led me off for a breather and a welcome fag. "Course I've had breakfast... honest!"

It happened to me for real once, nearly thirty years later at Horse Guards Parade

Ground in London at the 25th anniversary of the Falklands War. I'd travelled down to London with Mrs Riley, Andy Selby and his then wife Di. We met up with everyone at The Silver Cross Pub, just down from Trafalgar Square, all in our best suits with medals on our chests. Course we'd had the obligatory skinfull the night before, and, as standard procedure dictates, no breakfast! So before we all fall in for a very out of practice parade, it'd be rude not to have a few pints wouldn't it?

We met up with all of the familiar, (getting slightly older, faces) Knotty Ash, Blakey, Ste McGarry, John Fearon, Sid, Col, Foggy and the others. The same old stories come out about our times onboard but they never get boring, it's always a good laugh. We're all still the same really all these years later. Then there's a shout, a bloody loud Drill Sergeant type of shout that overrides the hum of chatter in the busy pub. The kind of scream that sounds like its coming from a man undergoing a delicate operation without anaesthetic. We all neck our beers quickly and rush out to the street. It's quite amusing forming up and marching now, being out of practice and 'tick-tock-ing out of step, when it was all so serious over thirty years ago in training. The hours on the parade ground all those years ago start to pay off and we start to look something like ex-service men. We're soon on our way, giggling and marching towards Horse Guards, with a grinning, red faced drill Sergeant screaming "EFF-RI, EFF-RI, EFF-RI, MARCH IN TIME YOU 'ORRIBLE LOT".

There was about two thousand of us veterans, all in formation, an amazing sight and it made me feel really proud.

Prince Andrew made a speech and was going on a little, if I'm honest and I wasn't really listening to him. I was taking in the atmosphere. Blah, blah, blah... and I'm wondering just how long he is going to go on for. On and on he goes. I can't make out where Cathy (Mrs Riley) is in the audience right over the far end... Ooh! I feel a little... ooh … a deep breath. On to tiptoes, wiggle toes... nope, it's not doing any good, a horrible wave of nausea washes over me. I really don't want to go down on a day like today. I've had no breakfast have I? I've had three pints, haven't I? This isn't good. The only thing to do is go down onto one knee. Down I go, Fearon's right behind me, "you alright Spike?" In a loud enough to hear whisper, "yep, I'll be fine". I was down there for a minute maybe, deep breaths, in through the nose, out through the mouth. I've got to get myself together… right... feeling better.

I stood up…

Unbeknown to me, the upward action combined with a restricted blood flow from being on one knee, resulted in me instantly blacking out and going down like a fucking nine pin! Backwards! Of course I was totally unaware of it.

"Ahhh, it's a shame isn't it? They're getting on a bit now". Am I dreaming? For some reason my eyes were shut, so I opened them. I was looking up the nostrils of two 1st Aiders, and there were two more carrying my feet. I was being carried away, face up, backwards out of the parade. "I'm OK! Put me down!" They insisted, and carried me all the way over to a tree at the edge of the parade ground and St James's Park, where I sat with some others that were void of breakfasts. Some we're stemming the blood flowing from nosebleeds, sustained from falling flat on their faces and drilling their noses straight into the asphalt.

I breathed in the cool fresh oxygen, laughing to myself and relieved that, thankfully, I was injury free. I sat there for a while looking around at everything going on.

Andrew brought his speech to an end, the sound of chinking medals and marching feet suddenly filled the air. Sid shouted out from the marching column containing my lot, "hey Spike! c'mon!" I got up and re-joined the marchers, got back into step and we marched all the way up the Mall to Buck House. The whole route was lined with crowds cheering and waving little Union Jacks on sticks, it was great.

John Fearon (I won't change his name, he wouldn't want me to) said that I just went down like a sack of shit, he'd seen it coming and actually managed to catch my head before it touched down!

The rest of the afternoon was spent swapping sea dits (sea stories) and boozing in The Cross, after a 'home-made' (pub kitchen) cheese burger and chips of course!

...

So the draft list said;

D181796F. RO2 (T) S. Riley - HMS Plymouth, Chatham Dock Yard.

I was also told that it was going to B.O.S.T. and Sea Trials, it was also going on a five or six month long deployment to the Windies (The West Indies). B.O.S.T. was something beginning with B then another word beginning with an O, the S&T was for sea trials.

Only I didn't hear it like that did I? I wasn't going to ask a silly question for fear of being slagged off as a twat, so off I went thinking I'd got the best draft ever. I was joining HMS PLYMOUTH, F126, Capt'n of the 6th Frigate Squadron! How cool was that?

I hadn't a clue actually, I thought I was going for Sea Trials in Boston! AMERICA! Wow! How lucky was I?

A little clarification came from Stevie McGarry who had also been drafted to the Plymouth. He filled me in about the Boston trip, I agreed with him, as if I already knew these finer details. It turned out later that B.O.S.T. was a very uncomfortable couple of weeks off Portland in rough seas, tearing up and down the coast, testing my throwing up skills which I'll explain in detail later. It also meant not much sleep and action stations practices. This was performed usually at a time when you were either trying to grab forty winks or eat. B.O.S.T. was also an acronym for Beginning of Sea Trials (6 weeks) and C.O.S.T. was Continuation of Sea Trials (2 weeks) - just the thought now of doing that again fills me with dread! It really wasn't any fun at all... well it may have been for some but it didn't do a lot for me. I felt pretty miserable most of the time. Perhaps I might have been a little more keen on it if I hadn't felt sea sick most of the time, because that feeling definitely puts a downer on just about everything.

"Spike! I like Spike!"

I left Mercury and drove home in my Triumph 1500 (metallic brown with a light brown vinyl roof. It suffered from terminal Triumph disease (galloping rust), the wheel arches crumbled like biscuits, so I bought some fibreglass wheel arches and riveted them on. It looked ridiculous with skinny tyres and white flared arches!) I'd swapped my Yamaha RD250 for it, and I took some leave up at home in Wombourne. I left the car at home and made my way by train to Chatham on the Sunday night. It was August 1980, I was nineteen and drafted! I made my way to Chatham by train and finally taxi, with my huge kit bag and grip (a two handled sports bag, a Pusser's grip was the one to have, made from Kaki cloth with leather handles. I didn't have one...) to the dockyard and HMS Pembroke. HMS Pembroke was the shore establishment attached to Chatham dockyard. At the main gate, I was given directions to find where I was billeted.

It looked like a very dismal place in the dark and drizzle, with large, dark, Victorian brick buildings looming overhead. I made my way down the main drag to my block. The block was named after some admiral or ship, (I can't ever imagine a future Naval Accommodation block being named 'Riley').

Feeling soaking wet, fed up and very alone, I knocked lightly on the door after double checking that I had come to the correct one, on the correct floor. I'd rather have just been at home, or even back on the parade ground of HMS Mercury. Quietly I opened the door expecting some tattooed, hairy arsed, sea dog to hurl a barrage of abuse at me for doing something wrong that I hadn't realised was actually wrong! Well I wish that was what had happened...

The room was pitch black, flavoured with a rancid stench hanging in the air that I couldn't quite place. Sweet and fruity to the discerning nose, but definitely rancid. To my left just inside the door I could see a bed with a bare mattress that had its fair share of DNA soaked into it. This must have been mine (the bunk not the DNA!). I reached for the bunk light on the wall and looked around in the dim glow it provided. A sleeping body lay in the bed next to mine, all around it was a dark damp looking colour, almost purple... was it blood? No, can't be, but this was definitely where the bouquet was coming from.

The figure stirred, swung its legs round and sat on the other side of the bed with its back to me. I stood motionless and watched as it stood up and swaggered over towards a white plastic chair on the far side of the room that looked like it had some clothes over the back of it. This bare arsed figure then proceeded to piss all over the chair and clothes. A voice screamed -"AAAARGH! KNOTTY! WHAT THE FUCK YA DOIN'?". It burbled something illegible, it, I assumed was called 'Knotty'. The lights came on and a very tired looking face fumed at him as he pushed him back towards his bed and said, "you've pissed all over me fuckin' uniform ya fuckin' twat!" I could then see other beds with body shapes stirring under the blankets and wardrobes in the room.

Knotty, an olive skinned, naked, skinny, hirsute person, with thick curly black hair, clearly pissed, then crashed obliviously back onto his bed and back into unconsciousness, squirming around in his purple stained sheets. I'd realised by now that the sheets had once been white and were now dyed with rum and blackcurrant puke! "Hi" said the tired face opposite, "I see you've met 'Knotty the piss head' already. I'm Sweeney". "Spike (I said), I won't ask", "yeah! Night Spike".

My eyes flickered open and I suddenly remembered last night's events. Sweeney was gone, his bed was made up with hospital corners and his damp clothes were missing too.

It woke up!

"Ooh...fuck...shit...what the? - oh yeah, ha ha!"

It looked at me through half closed eye slits, grinned a big toothy grin and said, "mornin!' I'm Knotty mate (he completely missed out the three t's). Don't think I'll drink that shit again, it don't make yer gob feel too good in the mornin'". And he sparked up a fag, using a Zippo lighter. (Well how was I to know this guy would end up being my best man and me his?!).

He showed me the way to the heads (bathroom) and after he'd bundled his purple foul smelling sheets up into a plastic bag, we went off to the dining hall for breakfast. The 'R. Ash' name tag above the pocket on his No.8's blue shirt gave me a clue as to how he got his nickname.

What a dump this place was! With long ancient corridors, peeling paint, crumbling plaster, no furniture... and cold! We got to the dining hall, a large room with plain furniture, and a big stainless range full of English. As we took our place in the queue, I watched the cockroaches running in and out of cracks and under the hygiene posters on the wall.

They were only little cockroaches about 1/2" long. The food wasn't too bad and I was introduced to Foggy Fothergill, Chalky Selby and Wee Stevie Windle.

By nine o'clock we were to be on board ship. I followed these guys down to the dockyard and there it was, well... a bit of an anti-climax to say the least! I saw the top half first, it looked old fashioned compared to the other ships like the sleek and fast Type 21's that others had been drafted to. It was in a bad state of repair with dockyard workers in overalls ferreting away on the upper deck, painting, welding, hammering and drinking tea. We came up to the edge of the dry dock... the hull was orange, which made it look a little peculiar. It looked huge out of the water and it was very un-nerving crossing the gangway with a good sixty foot drop under the planks. Once inside it was utter chaos, the deck was covered with plastic sheeting and duck boards. Duck boards being the operative word as you had to duck everywhere you walked to avoid splitting your head open on the exposed overhead brackets, pipes and ducting. Knotty, Steve, Chalky and Foggy lead me quickly through this passageway of dangling wires, cables and other obstacles, past aluminium, wooden and steel doors. I didn't have any time to peer into any of these compartments, all I did see were assortments of dials and complicated looking knobs, cables and switches in large grey-blue steel cabinets. Past the stainless steel counter and aluminium shutter of the galley and on towards the pointy end, down through a hatch and into the RO's mess (3E). It didn't look very homely at all, with a strong smell of paint and cigarette smoke. There was a fridge, a mirror, a TV, a Betamax video player, and a small table cluttered with mugs and beer tins.

A huge lump of a man was sat shirtless on the far side. He had been on duty on board last night, he was hunched over and sucking on a blue liner (R.N. cigarette) like his life depended on it. Sweeney was sat next to him in dry No 8's and Knotty introduced me to them as 'Spike'. The shirtless one held out his hand with a smile showing that his bottom teeth were in front of his top ones. He had shoulders you could sit on and a large gut (sorry mate!). "Hi, I'm Hutch" he said in a strong Glaswegian accent. I shook his hand. Everyone was sat down or lying on bunks, smoking and chatting. Steve McGarry came down the ladder, it was good to see a familiar face. Blue Liners by the way were the duty free cigarettes that smokers got stamps for every month. They were in a plain flat white folding packet and strong like Player's or Park Drive's with filters. Encouragement to smoke…

Steve and I were given lockers and keys. All of the lockers were in the far corner of the mess, twenty seven lockers corresponding with twenty seven bunks. The lockers were, at a guess, four feet tall and two feet wide... a tall door on the left for hanging clothes in and four drawers. All of your kit had to be stowed in there, there wasn't much room at all. The seating area called the 'mess square' was just two bottom bunks in the corner, enough to sit eight at a push. The bunks were all in banks of three, the top one hooked up and out of the way, the middle one folded down to form the back rest and the bottom bunk static as the seat. All available space was used up by bunks and lockers, the mess square was only about 8' x 8' and the whole compartment being approximately 20' x 15'. Hutch started dishing out orders and told Knotty to take me and Steve to the M.C.O. (the Main Communication Office).

Back up the ladder, then back down a few yards the way we had just come, past a varnished wooden ladder and to the aluminium, sound proofed, M.C.O. door. Inside it was a long compartment full of teleprinters on shelves, spewing out ticker tape. There were radios, tuning equipment and papers with a desk along the right hand side of the compartment. There was someone beavering away with papers and signals in the corner and a large bearded Radio Supervisor glanced round. Knotty said, "RS, here's RO Riley and RO McGarry". He looked at me with a grin and said in yet another Scottish accent (he only had one), "What's yoo're nehm?" (Strange question...) "Riley, RS", "No!" he said, "what's yer fur's nehm?". "Oh – Simon". He said "SIMON? What's yer nick-nehm?", "Spike", "Ha!" he said, "Simon's a poof's nehm - ahh don't like Simon, but SPIKE! - I LIKE SPIKE!" Thank God for that I thought, I'm glad he likes it! "Spike, I'm RS Wright (AKA: Shiner Wright, obviously a Chinese inspired nickname) and that's (pointing at the smaller bearded Chief Petty Officer at the desk) Chief Yeoman Doak" – he nodded. We left the room after Steve had been introduced as 'Steve' (obviously NOT a poof's name!) and Knotty gave us a guided tour of the whole ship that was to be home for the next eighteen months.

HMS Plymouth

I quickly got used to life onboard - it wasn't difficult as we were still in dry dock. I got used to my parts of the ship and, after a few days I knew how to get around.

My bunk was in the middle gulch, (a gulch is a space formed between two banks of bunks in a mess deck) it was the bottom bunk that was located next to a 3' wide vertical steel tube. This tube was put there so that I could stick pictures of my family on, photos of girlfriends went on the mess Gronk Board. The Gronk Board was basically a noticeboard with passport type photos pinned to it, displaying the conquests of mess members past and present (the uglier the better!). The tube was next to the hatch and the ladder, the only entrance / exit, there were neither windows nor port holes. It's worth noting here that ladders between decks were scaled facing the steps but always descended by facing outwards. You would usually raise your feet and control your descent with your grip on the aluminium tube handrails. Twenty seven blokes cooped up in there, drinking, smoking, burping, farting, puking and breathing - nice. A smell you just have to get used to, because you can't get a cabin unless you've got a double barrelled surname or you're called Rupert, although no one was of course... (A Rupert is a toffee nosed officer. For example, 'I walked into the Wardroom to nick an orange and it was full of Ruperts').

The hatch going up from the mess deck lead to the main drag, the corridor that lead through the ship from the pointy end to the arse end. Also known as 'The Burma Way'. As you poked your head out of the mess hatch, the NAAFI was right in front of you. When it was open the 'Can Man' would be behind the roller shutter and he was the main supply of Blue Liners (they were in a white packet with a blue line down the middle of the pack and a thin blue line down the cigarette), cold steak pies, crisps, cans of goffer (pop) and nutty bars (take a wild guess). Further to the right were the forward heads (toilets) to the left and the shower room to the right. The shower room was also known as the Dhobi Shack.

The heads were cleaned by whoever was on duty, they were clean-ish, but not a pleasant place to be. The 'trap' was entered via two little flappy doors, like saloon doors and there was always a porno mag stuffed away somewhere to while away five minutes or so. But otherwise whilst at sea, as I found out later, not the most comfortable place to take a dump. Being at the pointy end in 'Harry Roughers' (a bit of a swell) (a lot of words were prefixed with Harry, I don't know why, they just were! 'Harry icers' meaning 'freezing cold' for instance) meant that your relationship with being on an even keel at sea level and the peaks and troughs of waves could be a difference of... a lot! For example, imagine being sat there, Hustler in one hand, holding on for dear life, to stop yourself from levitating from the seat and cracking your bonce on the deck head (ceiling), not to mention the pipe work, as the pointy end rides the crest of a wave that's twenty feet high. Over the top of that wave is a deep trough, probably twenty five to thirty feet down. You're weightless for a couple of seconds, so is what you dumped in the pan. That meets your undercarriage half way back down. The nose continues down further until the buoyancy and the next wave that's breaking over the upper deck forces the front up again making you effectively double your weight as you go careering up to the top of the next 'girt goffer' (large wave), as we used to say. This gets repeated on and on and puts you off any sexual thoughts so you take a rain check and put the mag back!

Another thing, back then, I discovered the advantages of the 'front wipe' method. So you can do it sitting down, otherwise attempting to wipe whilst standing and twisted to reach with the Izal, as you clear a girt goffer could end in disaster, there's just not enough support. I've had many a deep and meaningful conversation defending the front wipe method in the pub before. But you just can't convince some people and I'm no longer entering the debate on that one, just do what you like - I don't care!

The Dhobi Shack was just opposite, it was a tiny compartment with a porthole at the far end, five or six sinks and mirrors to the right and two shower cubicles with no curtains to the left. There was a wire rack over the mirrors at head height for hanging your wet socks and pants and for keeping your towel dry. If you wore your towel it wouldn't do what it's solely designed for; drying you, as the water would splash out from the showers being used at full blast just a couple of feet away. So the routine was that you'd have to queue from the main drag and wait till you got in the door. Inside would be two or three waiting, and someone at each sink brushing their teeth and / or 'dhobying'. Dhobying means washing clothes, or 'going for a dhobi' meant 'going for a wash'. In fact, I've just looked it up and confirmed that a Dhobi is Hindi for a 'Washer man', so that's where that comes from. You'd have a plastic tube or tub filled with washing powder, aka 'dhobi dust', to wash your pants and socks. You took your turn at a sink, then jumped in a shower as soon as one became vacant. Once done, you collect your dhobying and put your towel back on as you get to the door. Then down the hatch back into the mess to finish off with 'foofs' (talc and antiperspirant). Having to dry your balls in front of seven or eight blokes who are trying to watch Debbie Does Dallas can raise its own problems. Empty fag packets, keys, pens and empty cans would be thrown in your general direction, the main target being your dangly tendrils.

On one occasion a new lad followed me into the shower room. Hutch squeezed in behind him - the room was full of steam and hot, with water splashing all over the place. I took my towel off and put it on the rack. I started my dhobying, filling the sink with hot water and dhobi dust. Hutch was stood there with his towel over one shoulder and his dhobi bag in one hand. He said to the new lad, who looked terrified as he clung to his towel like a condemned man, "get yer fuckin' towel off man! Ye'll get-et sooken wet man!" He looked at Hutch like a rabbit in the headlights as H pulled the towel free and flung it up onto the rack for him... releasing the biggest shlong I've ever seen... correction, I think anyone had ever seen... and I'm talking drooped in the natural state. Now I'd like to point out that, being male and having shared communal showers with other blokes, doesn't make me an expert on who's got a big-un, not that I'm interested, but this thing was enormous! He was mortified! Turned out he was a virgin, he was probably wondering why all these blokes had such tiny ones (in comparison). Unsurprisingly he quickly became legend and he was the best bloke to go out on the pull with, he'd get that bloody great thing out and the whole pub would go quiet! Briefly!

My bunk, tucked away down the gulch (normally a narrow and steep-sided ravine marking the course of a fast stream. In this case it was the space between rows of bunks), was the bottom of three, with three more adjacent, your mattress and sleeping bags were stowed away in dark red plastic covers. You had to make your bed or 'stow your pit' as soon as you got out of it, zipping it up into the covers so that it could be used in the unlikely scenario of a leak by stuffing it up against the bulkhead, shored up with wood to stop any water coming in from a hole in the hull (as if…). This was also where you'd keep your wank sock, or in my case an orange and black striped Wolverhampton Wanderer's bobble hat that my Gran had knitted for me! (I can't stand football by the way). You had to become expert at the art of pleasuring yourself without alerting anyone else to your activities. I actually managed to do it using the power of the mind alone. Now THAT requires a great deal of concentration and probably an equal amount of desperation at times!

The gulch behind mine was only separated by a thin steel partition with holes in it so discretion was very necessary. It was called a 'buggery board"... I don't even want to know why!... unless you were a certain Cornishman who used to just lie on his bunk in full view, ignoring complaints and just get on with it!

Anyway, under our hatch leading into the mess was another hatch under the ladder, on the deck that lead down to the 4.5" shell magazine below. Sleeping a deck above tons of high explosive didn't seem to bother any of us... not a jot! The tube I mentioned previously in this chapter - with all my photos stuck to it - turned out to be the hoist that hoisted the huge shells up to the double barrelled 4.5" gun on the upper deck. When that was in full swing it all made a hell of a racket!... I'll go into that later. At this time, in dry dock, I could have never imagined what it would be like.

The rest of the ship wasn't too difficult to navigate. Further forward was the diesel shack that housed two massive generators that were cleverly designed to assist those feeling seasick. The idea was, that when you just can't handle the nausea any more, you go towards the heads and smell the exhaust fumes leaking from the Jennies and that was guaranteed to make you see your cheesy hammy eggy again! I was particularly vulnerable when it came to seasickness, as was Admiral Lord Nelson of course! (Mental note to remember; 'The Lone Bean'). Beyond the Jennies was the paint store, right up in the very pointy bit, I would have had to have a bucket with me all the time if I had to work in there! Coming out of the mess hatch and turning left, you walked around the base of the four point five gun, containing all of the machinery for the huge double barrelled weapon on the upper deck. To the left there was a wooden varnished ladder leading up to the next deck, at the top it was left to the wheelhouse and the 'Jimmies' (1st Lt Iain Henderson's) cabin. To the right was the door to the ops room, a constantly darkened room with a green glow from the radar and sonar screens. To the right was the wheelhouse, a small compartment directly underneath the Captains seat on the bridge. A further ladder between the wheelhouse door and the ops room, continued up and emerged out onto the bridge, where my main part of ship was. In the corner, by the starboard bridge door, was a wooden desk with drawers, on top of that were the VHF & UHF radios. The bridge door led out onto the bridge wing - you walked down there to reach the base of the mast and the signal deck, where the flag lockers were at the end. The flag lockers were like large pigeon hole boxes, one on each side, near to the bottom of the mast. The halyard ropes were tied to cleats at the bottom of the mast. From there you could clip the alphabet, numbers and pennant flags from the flag locker, to the halyards and hoist them up the yardarms (the bits that stick out from the top of the mast). From there to the port side, to the ladder up to the signal deck where the four large reflector lamps or flashing lights, for sending Morse Code by light were. Two 10" and two huge 20" lights powered by Argon Arc rods (a bit like a welders torch and a mirror), and also the entrance to the mast.

The mast had a steel door and a small store room for flags about six feet square, called the Visual Signals Store. There was a ladder up the centre of the mast, with a smaller compartment above and two smaller ones above that. An excellent hide out, specifically designed for eating pies in and for sleeping on flag bags. It was also where Tommy Doak, the Chief Yeoman, our boss, kept what he called his 'white man's magic' which consisted of a yellow

Puch racer and a bag of golf clubs. More of that later.

Rear of the mast was the funnel, Captains Sea Boat on the port side and the Sea Rider, a fast rigid inflatable on the Starboard side. After that, past the funnel, down a set of steps and along towards the rear where the helicopter hangar and flight deck was. After that more steps down to the quarter deck and mortar barrels. From there you can head forwards again inside, up the main drag that took you past the sick bay, scribes office, after PO's mess, dining hall, galley, main signals office (MCO) and back to the ladders leading up to the bridge again. All along that route, were hatches leading down a deck to other mess decks. Most were a little bigger than our RO's mess, there was also the Wardroom, the officer's cabins and the Captain's cabin off the Ops room.

Underneath all that were the engine and boiler rooms, places I never ventured into much. There were, I'm pretty sure, about two hundred and twenty men onboard, this was a few years before WRENS were allowed to go to sea

We were gradually getting the ship into ship-shape condition, living in the shore-side accommodation and spending time off going into Chatham drinking in the 'dive bars'.

Chatham dockyard was a series of basins, separated from the Medway River by massive locks. Because we were in a dock, we couldn't use the heads onboard (just imagine the unlucky dockyard worker working in the bottom of the dry dock), so we had to use the heads ashore which was quite a trek when you'd got a bladder full in the middle of the night, it'd be cold too. This is where the piss buckets came into use. Massive buckets were put in the heads so that you could have a piss during the night. I remember you'd turn up to empty your bladder and the bucket would be 'toppers' with piss and quite often the cherry on the cake would be a bloody great floater bobbing around too! Those buckets must have held over five gallons of piss! I wonder if this is where the term 'take the piss' comes from? Of course we'd have to take it in turns to empty the bloody things. So two of you had to lug this bloody great bucket of piss and try your best not to slop too much along the main drag as you struggled with it all the way to the gangway and ashore, oh the smell!

We were also able to draw three cans of beer - Courage-per man per day, one to be consumed at lunch time and the other two in the evening although that was never kept to of course and you could always swap or save cans. We even got a dockyard worker to create some hiding places for us to stow beer under the seating in the mess square. We even used to stick them in the air vents to save for special occasions. You had to put your ticket in whether you wanted beer or not, there would always be someone who wanted more than three in any case. There was a pipe over the Tannoy system just before lunch "BEER IS NOW READY FOR COLLECTION, DUTY MESSMEN MUSTER AT THE BEER STORE".

New Romantics.

Fashion-wise, I didn't know where the fuck I was! (between trends, I suppose). It was coming towards the end of 1980, 'New Wave' was beginning to take over from the Punk Scene, as was 'Ska', with lyrics like; 'you done too much, much too young, you're married with a kid when you should be having fun with me', an apt song for those days, another very apt song, because after a skinfull, you'd often find yourself wandering around a; 'Nightcluuub, what am I doing here? Nightcluuu-ub - watching the girls go by - spending money on - BEER!'

I'd joined the Navy almost a year earlier and I had come from an engineering apprenticeship, I was a biker and I had a blue Yamaha RD250B. Me and Neal 'Wally' Walters used to travel down to HMS Mercury on our motorbikes. His was an RD250A, with a very odd sounding second gear. We used to communicate with each other by flashing headlights or brake lights, depending who was in front. Whizzing through the Cotswolds one time, I got a puncture in my back tyre, on the way down the huge hill that used to bring you into Broadway Village (there's a ring road around it now) I wobbled straight into the gravel trap and left the bike stood up on its own. It was sunk up to the engine in gravel, while we went to the local Nick for help, which they didn't. We ended up finding a garage that sold an emergency puncture repair kit and I wobbled home.

Before joining, I had shoulder length, limp blonde hair with a middle parting and I was into Rush, Iron Maiden, Led Zep, etc. All the heavy rock bands, most of which I'd been to see at The Reading Rock Festival 1980 and Knebworth '79. Now I was having to get my head, sorry, my very short haired head around this new scene.

My hair was now short back and sides with a middle parting, with the beginnings of spikes appearing (hence my nickname) not as cool as Paul Weller's barnet and I was having to get used to wearing slightly more up-to-date clothes. Frilly cuffs on shirts (see Spandau Ballet), Tukka Boots (see Puss in Boots) and zoot suit jackets (see Humphrey Bogart) from second hand shops. This look was rounded off with a pair of Oxford Bags (see Bogey again). The fringe was the next instalment. Essential then, especially for a Matelot who wasn't allowed to grow his hair but what was under your cap was yours! Then gel! Thank the fucking Lord for hair gel, limp hair was no more. Cue; proper spikey hair. You ran the risk of being labelled as being 'queer' for all of these fashion ideas, but it was cool and trendy at the time so we took no notice, we knew what we were doing and we always had money in our pockets for 'runs ashore'.

Sometimes we'd get stopped by the Killick Regulator, or the Master at Arms on the gangway who'd refuse to let us go ashore 'dressed like a fucking pooftah!' On one occasion, I had to stand still at the top of the gangway, while the Master at Arms turned my collars down and rolled the sleeves of my jacket back down before he let me go down the gangway, "that's better, you see? Much smarter". He obviously wasn't down with the kids. Then on the quay, I'd stick my earring in and pick up my winklepicker boots from the jetty having tossed them overboard earlier. We'd go to discos and the dances of the time would be perfected. You had to do it right, although standing and just swaying a little, with the fringe resting over one eye was pretty cool too. Knotty Ash and Wee Stevie Windle were the ones leading the way in this department. Foggie Fothergill, me and Chalky not far behind.

I'm sure we looked pretty good (for then...) and the pulling of birds results were pretty good. We were always better than the Stokers and Seamen at pulling (birds). Some of the others used to break free from their old fashioned restrictions and take the risk of being slagged off by their own mess mates and go ashore with us lot on the pull. You know who you are (Scotty Ronald & Garry Borthwick). They were good times, Duran Duran were starting out with their early hits. Bauhaus were really deep and mysterious... if you knew their songs then you knew your stuff. The music that was still underground was the best because it was of the same genre, and the more of those lesser known songs you knew the words to, the cooler you were really. I loved The Cure and their early stuff, 'Saturday Night' and 'A Forest'. Some say the music of the '80's was rubbish... Rubbish! All the stuff I used to listen to on my Sony Walkman cassette player was still the heavy and progressive stuff like Pink Floyd (The Wall), Van Halen, Thin Lizzy, Boston, Rush... the list goes on.

Serious girlfriends were a little thin on the ground in those days, I think we spent more time perfecting the art of drinking heavily in The Dive Bars in Chatham 'till late , working odd hours and then going back home at the weekends. That lifestyle kind of scuppered any long term relationships. I wasn't very patient in those days when it came to girls and their many needs, so they didn't last long.

It's no wonder really that we constantly had to shake off the "ooh hello sailor" jibes, we didn't do ourselves any favours... but we were having a great time and we were most definitely straight. Perhaps we didn't quite look it but who did in the Eighties'? (Alright - Motörhead did).

At Sea.

I'd been to sea before in the twenty foot family boat when I was younger, so I had experienced - and suffered - seasickness from bobbing around like a cork. I wasn't worried about going to sea in a four hundred and fifty foot Warship.

The day came early 1981, I think, when we left Chatham Docks and headed out into the Medway... fine, no probs, it was quite alright. I was getting used to working and passing signals back and forth to other ships. Using flashing lights and flags to send signals, painting things on the upper deck and scrubbing decks. Everything I'd imagined since Wally's big brother Steve (RIP), recommended the life in 'The Andrew' to us. Chipping and painting in the sunshine, waving to the girlies in the tour boats and getting a tan.

But there was this strange feeling I always had whenever I went to sea. A taste in my mouth, made worse by smoking Blue Liners, which rarely went away whenever I was at sea. It took my appetite away, I don't know if anyone else had that, but I had to force dry bread down me to try to soak up the bile in my stomach and, as much as I wanted a beer, having a few tins in the mess with the lads when there was a swell was completely out of the question! I'd have been breathing in those diesel fumes and blowing chunks all over the latest copy of Rustler in no time.

One of the occasions that Knotty never lets me forget was when I'd been suffering a bit with seasickness. Normally, I could handle it. I'd be on the bridge, and I'd say to the Officer of the Watch "permission to throw up Sir?" He'd say "yes please", and I'd open the bridge door, sometimes with great difficulty as wind and rain would come blustering through as you're pushing it open. As you go through, the door would slam shut with the wind, one clip would secure it. Then I'd hang on to a ten inch lantern, and hurl over the side. I actually got used to it! On this occasion, I was on watch and I'd been chucking up for hours, the Roughers was relentless and it wasn't going to die down over the next few days either... I was feeling really ill. People do actually turn green at sea... I know I did! Chalky was just as bad as me, he actually did turn the actual colour of green once! The Officer of the Watch got Knotty out of his pit to take over from me, as I needed to get my head down. He was made to clean up the mess I'd left, where the wind had carried my Corn Dog Hash all over the life rafts. He arrived on the bridge and gave me a wide berth to avoid contamination, and I silently slid down the ladder to find the sanctuary of my pit.

He wasn't very happy about cleaning up after me and, when I eventually re-surfaced, he let me know about his task of cleaning up the contents of my stomach.

We were looking over the side the next day and that's when we saw it... The lone bean! Teetering on the edge of a 30' abyss, void of any signs of tomato sauce, just sitting there. I think he just gave up in the end and leapt into the sea to end it all. The bean that is, not Knotty. We're still good mates! (me and Knotty that is...).

So, I discovered that anything from a force three or four up to a gale force nine was the puking zone for me, anything either side of that I was fine! The rougher the better, the smoother even better, but in the middle, mmmmb? mmmmmmb! Sea sickness was something I just had to get used to, there was no bloody choice really.

We went straight into sea trials, which was an eye opener for a sprog like me, and the rest of us who hadn't done it before. They reckoned that it was a simulation of war. Now the thing is - up to this point, there hadn't been a war apart from Suez and The Cold War that, as far as I knew, was just cold! In reality, the chances of going to war were pretty remote. I do have to say that I joined for the life, not for the 'going off to war' part. I didn't fancy that in the slightest! Although we were training to be proficient at it, nothing was further from my mind at the time, it was horrendous! If this is what war is like I'm not playing!! (I obviously knew fuck all back then!).

We were put through the mill. We were battered from pillar to post with fire drills, man overboard drills, evasive manoeuvres (usually performed at scran times (meal times), which would often result in twenty of us sliding across the dining hall and ending up in a big snotty heap in the corner, covered in scran!). There were simulated air attacks, submarine attacks and IRA terrorist attacks when alongside or at anchor.

Sleep was at a premium. We'd be working shifts or 'watches', which would be six hours on and six hours off, although you'd still have to work through the day for eight hours.

The Forenoon was 08:00 - 12:00.

The Afternoon was 12:00 - 16:00.

The 1st Dog was 16:00 - 18:00.

The Last Dog was 18:00 - 20:00.

The First was 20:00 - 00:00 midnight.

The Middle was 00:00 - 04:00.

The Morning was 04:00 - 08:00.

You'd occasionally get an afternoon off, known as a 'make and mend', dating back to when sailors mended their kit and the sails after you had done the middle watch the night before. I used it mainly for sleeping (thank the Lord for Dhobi Wallahs and engines!). The six on six off watches were the worst as it would drag endlessly. One of those watches was when I discovered that it is actually possible to fall asleep looking through binoculars whilst stood up, having them pressed against the windscreen between your eyes and the glass. The quality and duration of the sleep is severely impaired though! I mean, you've got to be extremely shattered to be able to do that!

During official sleep, the alarm for action stations would sound, and I'd leap out of bed and run up to the bridge and be at my action station in front of the radio on the bridge, with pen in hand and headphones on within two minutes. (That was reduced to 1:30 for real, more about that later).

At the weekend we'd normally come into Portland Harbour near Weymouth, and if we weren't going 'Harry Homers' (home) on 'weekenders' we'd hit the town. I really can't remember much about our runs ashore in Weymouth. We would go ashore, (pick up our cool stuff), a couple of pints later we'd be well on the way to being totally 'rat legged'. We used to say we were going on a 'Rabbit Run' that would be buying gifts or souvenirs. Alternatively a 'Postcard Run' which involved Postcards (I know – deep!) Either way you'd inevitably lose whatever you bought before getting back onboard.

I do remember having the common sense once, in The Harbour Club (a disco on the front), by pulling Knotty backwards out of there, in order to make a quick exit. Foggy had got involved in some pushing and shoving. Knotty (pissed as a fart), thought it would be a good idea to twat Foggies' assailant on the head with his dimple pint pot. Neither pot nor head broke and no injury was caused but it was time to get out of there, as everyone piled in and fists started to fly. Now I'm not a fighter, and being outnumbered by angry civvies, also armed with pint pots, wasn't a situation I was prepared to get involved in.

I got mixed up in a scrap once that wasn't very nice, I had only just joined The Mob and I was still in training at HMS Raleigh... I was eighteen. It was really an assault and it was planned too! Me and Wally had driven home for the weekend and we were in a pub in Kingswinford... The Bell it was called (the one they knocked down and re-built). We were with another older lad called Trev, and there were some lads sat down in a semi-circular seating area just back from the bar that I noticed didn't look right. You know when you can tell someone's staring at you? They looked a little out of place. I hadn't seen them before. I used to go in there before I joined up... long haired, I never saw any trouble in there. It's funny how you remember little things, but I remember saying out loud over the noise of chatter and music, "she's as rough as a bear's arse". I was talking to Wally and I was referring to a singer on the juke box that was playing... can't think who. Anyway, we were at the bar, we picked up the three pints and turned round to find a seat. We squeezed in, me and Wally sparked up a cigarette each, when a voice said, "I 'eard yow say moy mate's as roof (say it like woof) as a bears arse". I looked round in the direction of the Black Country voice and saw a short, stocky lad, about seventeen. He was staring at me. He looked like he was verging on being a skinhead but not a fully-fledged one, with short hair, but not a skin head. He had nice new, red 18 holed Dr Martens on though. He was sat with six or seven other lads, all teenagers, with leather biker jackets and long hair. Normally a situation I'd be comfortable in, I'm a biker for fuck sake, so what should I be worried about? I said "I was on about (I remember now) Stacy Lattisaw". This explanation fell on deaf ears, the bikers looked angry... I missed my long greasy hair. He grabbed my pack of twenty Players No6 and crashed them to his mates. I looked at one, who looked at me and smiled at me as he lit his buckshee cigarette, looking very pleased with himself. They were obviously looking for an excuse for a fight.

I just hate that attitude that some young thugs seem to revel in. They have already sized you up and made the decision that they could pick a fight with you and the chances are they'd win. That way they can brag to their mates about how they were involved in a scrap, then explain an edited version of an argument and the fight that ensued. If a bookie was involved they'd be odds on favourite, with little risk to their health and safety.

The situation made us feel uncomfortable, so we decided to leave. As I said I'm not a fighter, and without any formal training in that department, apart from cushion boxing with my little brothers Dave and Paul, I didn't think I had a chance against a hard little shit like him, who was probably well or at least more practiced at the art of fist scrapping than I was. So on a nod we necked our beers and left. As we walked down the street, towards The Cross Inn about three hundred yards down the road, I heard, as Paul Weller would say, "The rumble of boots, the smell of brown Ieva". Well I did have a little money but no takeaway curry, and I wasn't married, but the confrontation was on us pretty quick. The 'rough as a bears arse' comment was raised briefly, followed by a punch in the face, my nose and upper lip taking the impact, "Goo on, foight 'im then!" the leather jackets were saying, but the risk seemed too great.

There were three or four behind him and I thought they'd just join in and kick the shit out of me if I fought back. I could see Wally with a couple of the bikers who were kicking and punching him. Trev was further down the road, negotiating with another one. I couldn't understand the mentality of what was going on. Why? What was he trying to prove? All of this in a few seconds, then another punch towards my stomach... I moved... he punched the fence instead. That gave him a good excuse to get angry, so he piled in. I was arms and hands out trying to protect myself against the blows coming in, while my knees were slowly giving way underneath me... then it stopped. The little git held his hand out and pulled me to my feet, HIS FUCKING BUS HAD PULLED UP!! They all got on and the bus pulled away! They actually said "Bye".

My top lip was developing an advanced trout pout and my nose was streaming blood and snot, Wally was in a similar state. We walked around the corner to the local Cop Shop and I was told off by the Desk Sergeant for dripping blood on his counter!

Nothing ever came of it, hence the term I've heard so many times since; 'Coppers never do fuck all'. It would involve some protracted investigation in order to apprehend the perpetrators of that case! Far too much work for him and his men who obviously had bigger fish to fry than the local yobs from Pensnett.

Thinking back, I was a bit of a poof wasn't I? I should've done this, I should've done that. You always kick yourself afterwards, convinced that, if you could rewind, you'd have fought back like an angry Bruce Lee! So, for nights after that, fuming over having to drink soup through a straw. I'd go over the situation in my head and imagine how I should've held his arm when he hit the fence, and, with his head still lowered, a right to the temple and he goes down, then, face his mates and say (blag) "c'mon then? Next??" Hindsight eh?

It seemed like we were there (Portland Sea Trials) for ever, but the promise of going to the West Indies (AKA; Windies) on a six month deployment was all we needed to spur us on, although that was still a year off.

Once we finished with the sea trials we went on a few jollies; Brest, Malmo, Guernsey and other bloody freezing places. We anchored off in Guernsey and had what was called Cinderella leave (you can work that one out yourself), because we had to be ferried by liberty boat from ship to shore. Booze was really cheap but we had to go back onboard just as it was getting interesting.

Malmo was good though, we were given the freedom of the town. We had a posh lunch with the Mayor. Stevie Mac and me had the task of raising a Union Flag from a balcony in the town square. We were pissed as farts after too many free glasses of wine at the lunch. How we ever managed to remember at which note by a bugler we had to raise the flag, I'll never know! Although I do vaguely remember some Army bloke explaining two or three times. Beer was really expensive too, about as much as it is now for Christ sake! The quality of porn in the heads increased substantially after that visit.

The months went by and we became Captain of the 6th Frigate Squadron and we were to be based in Rosyth, rather a long way from home! Rosyth was a very... is a very cold and windy place. Edinburgh was nice. We used to go there to stock up on clothes and get haircuts, then head for Rose St, a half mile long street lined with pubs... what could be better than that? You'd inevitably get back onboard with a lot less 'Rabbits' than you had started out with. 'Gizzits' are similar to 'Rabbits' but obviously 'Buckshee'! (Do you follow?) Then as you're trying your best to act sober, walking up the main drag, the Reggie, (The Killick Regulator - Taff. He was and probably still is Welsh, was not up to speed with current trends) would shout "GET THAT FUCKING EARRING OUT, YOU'RE ON A FUCKING WARSHIP YOU FUCKING BROWN HATTER!" I of course didn't say; "I'm sorry but that's homophobic and I take offence at that sort of language, you have made me feel harassed, alarmed and distressed. Besides, I'm not gay!"

Instead, on hearing that, I quickly took my earring out, scuttled off to my bunk to get some zeds in and said nothing.

I always wondered if Taff thought that the weight of wearing an earring must have caused the left side of your head to bow down, (you couldn't have one in the right ear in those days, to balance it out, because wearing one in both ear lobes really did mean that you were gay! Even gays didn't do that then, they just kept it to the right ear. I don't know who invented those rules!) Taff was obviously unaware that you can't actually 'feel' an earring and it's easy to forget that you're wearing one. Or was he just keeping us on our toes? The latter I think! Unless of course his missus had difficulty in raising her head up due to the weight of a pair of dangly ones!

We'd get 'big eats' from a chip van on the way back to the dock yard that did chips and beans in a plastic tray. We used to stock up on stodge there after most runs ashore. I argued with the bloke once because he had dirty fingernails, he told me to "FUCK OFF" and I went hungry. I don't think he recognised me the next time I went. It's not there now, I know because I organised a reunion for all our Jock friends in 2013 and could have murdered big eats. Everything is shut in Rosyth by midnight now, and fuck, does it rain in Rosyth??

I had the honour of raising the Jack on the focsle (pointy end, fo'c's'le or forecastle...) as we came into any port, which was fine in most places but, in the Firth of Forth, under those bridges in a sailor suit? Bloody freezing, the wind up there goes straight through you! If you look at a sailor suit, you'll note that it is made out of black woollen material, has a V neck with the blue collar over the shoulders. Under the V neck is a cotton square necked T shirt called a white front. There is no seal around the neck and it offers absolutely NO wind or cold protection at all. Icy wind would find its way down the front of that little number, freezing your upper half, only stopped by your belt. You do of course have the white sailor hat, the top is plastic and waterproof, but it is specially designed to catch the wind under the rim. So in high wind, just to make you feel even more uncomfortable, a handy cotton strap is available to put under your chin, just to restrict your breathing a little, clever eh?

Standing there at a lean towards the wind and rain means you have to get used to your balls heading up through your abdomen seeking warmth, only to be stopped by your belt!

Once the first rope goes over a bollard, you then raise the flag. Quickly but evenly up the flagstaff, it mustn't touch the ground, (an offence made punishable by death) it MUST be the right way up (getting that wrong would be a shitty death) and it must run up the runners in the pole smoothly with no snags. If it's upside down, the main giveaway is that it won't reach the top of the pole because the Inglefield Clip (a small 'C' shaped brass clip, for joining the ropes together) gets stuck and it looks like it's at halfmast. So you don't have to be a smart arse who knows which way up a Union Jack should be - if it doesn't reach the top, it's upside down!

Often at sea the weather would be absolutely horrendous and, compared with modern equipment that keeps you warm these days, our kit was shite... all you could do was layer up.

One night we all decided to go into Dunfermline on the piss. The plan was to go to The Princess Club (I think it was called), they had male strippers on, on a Monday night, bear with me on this one... It was full of women! The no-neck, overcoated, bulldog licking, piss-off-a-thistle-faced-bouncer, (take a breath!) who probably thought we were gay anyway, let us in. It worked a treat... we walked out with a wee birdy each. Me and Knotty had an adjoining old fashioned shop doorway each (the recessed type), and the snogging and groping of respective ladies commenced. There was chanting in the distance..."lah lah lah-lah laah, (quiet at first and getting louder) "we hate the Eng'lesh! "..."WE HATE THE ENG'LESH!"...Shit! I thought they might just carry on by, if we stayed shtum. My plan was working until Knotty (the twat), stepped out of his recess onto the pavement, right in front of them, looking like the Dandy Highwayman. Instead of saying 'STAND AND DELIVER!" he says "OI WHAT THE FACK ARE YOU ON

ABAAT YA SILLY CANT'S?" (A moth farted in the Kirkcaldy).
"ENG'LEEEEHHSH MAAAN - GET HEM!"
Knotty realising he's just poked a very short stick in a very big hornets' nest, set off running, leaving his bird, me and my bird just stood there. Four or five blokes went running off after him. I was stood there in disbelief as the rest suddenly realise 'there's an'er wan!' Three of them turned and looked at me, lipstick smudged on my face (not mine...), stood next to one 'o their birds from their toon. Fists clenched, as did my buttocks.

A little outnumbered (as per usual), I ran across the road as a taxi pulled up, I went onto the pavement and tried to open the back door, of the Ford Granada. Before I could open it the driver managed to reach the popper and locked the fucking doors! BANG! *******, a punch on the back of my head. The two girls were there, as I was trying to fend these lads off, the wee lassies were screaming like blue murder! "Get aaafah hem ya wee shite ye!" One grabbed my shirt, ripping the buttons off and snapping my silver chain, completely missing my chest hair as it hadn't appeared yet fortunately. My chain had a fish bone pendant and a silver cross. Pushing, shoving and missed punches to and fro. One of the girls shouted at the driver to open the door, which he did. Luckily, they began to give up and wander off into the direction of where Knotty had gone. The three of us got in the taxi, he turned it around and we went after him. The brave lads of Dumf's had disappeared and the Dandy Highwayman appeared from the shadows, with a ripped Bowie Jacket and a grazed knee. He got in the cab and said that he ran off but the smooth soles on his Tukka Boots made him slip on the wet road and he fell down. They started laying into him but, unfortunately, (and I mean that most sincerely folks!), they hadn't done much damage. What a bloody eejit! I went back up there the next day to see if I could find my lucky fish... I was unlucky. I found the cross and a bit of chain trodden into the tarmac but that was it. Why do certain members of the public think it's necessary to beat people up for no apparent reason? Never even thought of Racism back then...

When the weather was really bad at sea and you were on duty on the upper deck, it was pretty nasty, wet and cold. Wind and spray would swirl around you, making it very difficult to take notes with pen and paper when trying to read a Morse signal to communicate with other ships by flashing light or flag signals.

Hours and hours spent on the signal deck, exposed to the elements, made going down below decks to scavenge for tea a welcome break. The trouble was, it didn't last long enough. You would have loved to watch Debbie Does Dallas on the Betamax for the twentieth time in the warm, down in the mess, but it was always very difficult to get all the necessary ingredients together to make a round of teas. Anyway, I did have my sources for scavenging... places like the Wardroom or one of the Stewards if there was one around... they were always good for scrounging little luxuries from. There was always fruit on the Wardroom table too... so snaffling an orange or an apple in the middle of the night was a risk worth taking. Their bananas always lasted longer than ours did for some strange reason! I got the tea making stuff together, watched Debbie for ten minutes, then made my way back up to the signal deck with four plastic cups of tea.

Now I had my excuse for the taste of the tea already worked out... we'll its dark down there!... and when it's dark, it's very difficult to tell the difference between sugar and salt! I battled my way up there, presented the hot teas to my welcoming customers and waited…

"Spike yer fuckin eejit! You've put salt in the fuckin' tea! Go get mer tea, wi' fuckin' shoogar en!" I got back down to the mess for the library scene, took me ages to find the sugar...

We had 'foulies'... or foul weather waterproof jackets and trousers, but when it was cold, you'd have your uniform on with a pair of jeans and a civvy jumper on underneath. Sometimes in really rough seas, even up on the signal deck, we would get soaked from waves coming over us. The bow would dip deep into the trough of a wave and a wall of solid green water would rise up with broken up white frothing water on the top. The green water would smash into the 4.5 turret and the bridge windows, the rest would shatter into billions of droplets and splash over us. And we were a good forty feet up from the waterline! Not to mention a good hundred feet from the front! Hence the term 'shipping it green'.

Fortunately, inside the ship the temperature was always a constant nice and warm. Even so, when you had a chance to climb into your pit, you'd be in there like a shot. As any nineteen to twenty year old kid knows, you need sleep and lots of it! Sleep was one thing we didn't get enough of for our liking. On the other hand, when the weather was nice, I really was living the dream and working on the upper deck in the sunshine... there's always something to paint grey on a warship, although never in the shade. If you were painting on the starboard side and the ship turned so that the sun was shining on the port side, then it was time to start painting on the port side!

Bunting Tosser.

My job as a Radio Operator was a 'tactical' RO, which meant that rather than fiddling with radios, tuning them and reading high speed Morse Code. I was more involved with visual communications in the form of flags and flashing light. So, after ten weeks General Communicator training, we then did another thirteen weeks specialising as Tactical Radio Operators at HMS Mercury, in Petersfield. I decided to go down the tactical route, following Steve's advice and remembering 'chipping and painting on the upper deck, and of course, waving at the girlies'. So I learned to type and learned to read Morse rather than listening to it. I was struggling at twelve words per minute listening to it and it was only going to get faster, up to sixty or seventy wpm. The limit of reading Morse by light was about ten words per minute, so that was a bonus for me. Little did I realise at the time that reading and writing down a message sent to you by a ship in the distance, with the sun behind it, or in a force nine gale, holding on to stop wind and rain washing you off the duckboards, was arguably even more difficult! Ideally there would be two of you, one reading and operating the light and the other writing down the message... ideally being the operative word. Then you'd go back onto the bridge looking like a drowned hippy at a Glastonbury festival and try to read the message to the Skipper from a sopping piece of message paper that was breaking up in your numb fingers. Your Chinograph pencil has long given up and with everything else the message hadn't been committed to memory." "Sir! Message from the, err…" He'd say, "Yes Riley, Chief Doak has given me the message, thank you". I'd slop my soggy arse back down at the desk and try to warm up! Tommy Doak... no doubt behind me sniggering in his beard and remembering when he had gone through exactly the same thing when he was a young sprog.

There was a VHF radio, a 2002 I think it was, it had a red LED light, that flicked left and right, covering two channels, ch16 – the emergency channel and another depending on where you were. It was under the windscreen on the desk for communicating with other ships, Harbour Masters and tugs etc. There was UHF radio for short distance communication with other warships, there was the 'Bridge Log' for noting all of the comings and goings of messages, that was to come in very useful for part of this book later on. There was also a little 5" Aldis lantern stowed away in a little metal box to my right on the bulkhead near the door to the bridge wing, which is where the 10" lantern was mounted. It had louvre type shutters inside, operated by a handle on the right side, there was a sight with cross hairs and a handle on the side for aiming at your correspondent up to a few miles away. They were recycled and dated 1942. They'd probably seen some action. There was another Aldis and ten inch on the port side. There were two more ten inchers on the signal deck, with two Argon Arc powered twenty inch reflectors that you could use to (just about on a good day) send a message to a ship twelve miles away on the horizon. Sometimes you could only just see the top half of a ship on the horizon, the hull would be obscured by the curvature of the earth, and you could still see the flickering light from there. The RO twelve miles away on a twenty incher would have a similar view (obviously!).

Just below the signal deck on each side were the flag lockers, as I said earlier, where all of the alphabetical and numerical flags were stowed along with the pennants that could be hoisted up to the yardarms from there. All the International and spare flags were stowed in sacks in the mast (pillow shaped), so all of the flags and codes were learnt, that was an ongoing process, there was quite a lot to it.

Other duties were to work in the MCO (Main Communications Office) down below, and that was usually manning the broadcast, which was a teleprinter that spewed messages out on carbon copy paper from a roll which had to be ripped off the printer and distributed accordingly. The messages were classified, from NATO secret, down to un-classified, and needed to be passed to the recipient as a 'Routine message', which was a snail's pace, up to a 'Flash message', which was like yesterday! That was the 'Message Handling' part of the job. It was around this time that the Navy phased out the old Gestener Copier machines. Perhaps, I don't know for sure, but some sailors used to use the chemical liquid ('Ormig Juice') that the machines had to be topped up with for drinking! They went with the new Xerox copiers. The problem with these new-fangled machines was that the ship would roll about while you were copying a message and only half of the page would print because the toner had shifted in the drum. I wonder if they've overcome that little glitch yet.

I remember one such message, probably THE most important message we ever received on the ship was the one where Charles & Di announced their sprog being born and Tug Wilson I think it was, missed it! At the top of the page it said "SPLICE THE MAINBRACE!" In English that meant; 'break out the rum!' Tug obviously didn't know what it meant and ditched the message in the bin. It wasn't until a few days later when someone found out that we should've all had a tot of rum ration, poor Tug wasn't the most popular RO onboard for a while!

That was the job in a nutshell. Obviously there are no cleaners on board so everyone has to do their bit, scrubbing and polishing floors and brass bits, cleaning the bogs and 'spitkids' out.

Spitkids (apparently aka; 'spitkits', and also a word for a small boat), were horrendous aluminium bowls about two feet in diameter that usually contained a drop of beer that would douse cigarettes. Originally designed for spitting in (tobacco?) but horrendous none the less. One would be placed on the floor in the middle of the mess square. We didn't used to spit in them... that was pretty disgusting, using them as an ashtray was bad enough.

Cleaning was a job that was manically done. With Captains rounds or Officer of the Watch rounds every evening at about

7pm, where anyone not on watch had to clean their part of ship, i.e. the mess or part of the deck of the Main Drag, or the heads and shower room. At seven, the Captain or OOW would tour the ship, some of the more fastidious would wear white gloves (dust detectors). Everyone not on duty would be dressed in No 2's (a sailor suit), and you'd have to stand to attention at the alert of a bosun's call (a whistle) for the inspection. All a bit of a pain in the arse really but, on reflection, very necessary (a clean ship is a happy ship, so they say...).

I should perhaps explain the uniform. No.8's were working rig... blue cotton trousers and a blue cotton shirt, a white patch above the left breast pocket with your name on and a badge on your right arm, showing your trade. The more faded your shirt, the more 'Jack the Lad' you were. Mine was two crossed flags with a star above, indicating that I was a first class bunting tosser! A beret with an anchor badge and a pair of steaming bats, which were ugly lace up steel toe capped boots. It was important to look 'Jack' (the Lad), because this was an unofficial seniority indication. Things like a beard and tattoos were obvious, a big scar down your cheek and a hook would have been a little OTT. A faded No.8 shirt or an older issue one was a good indication. You could of course have your hair tarred. No-one would have had that done, although I did meet an old ex-matelot with two teeth once... I won't mention his name, ha ha!... but he did actually have his hair tarred at one point, unbelievable!

No.1's were your best sailor suit with gold braid badges. Older salty sea dogs would have the horizontal creases in their trousers, five or seven creases spaced at the width of your pay book, depending if you were a short arse or taller for the seven creases. It was so that you could fold them flat rather than hanging them on a hangar to save space... I just had the newer plain vertically creased flared bottom trousers. The white front and jacket with the blue collar and the helicopter landing pad... sailor's hat.

No.2's were more your everyday suit the same as No.1's but with red badges.

There was also the tropical kit or No.6's that I never wore. Now THAT was camp looking. A white sailor suit with white canvas shoes and socks! Christ! They made you look like Laurence of Arabia goes to sea!

There were lots of other items and everything was referred to as 'Pussers' if it was Navy issue, for example, a Pussers belt, a Pussers grip, a Pussers rum ration and Pussers bog roll that had 'HM SHIPS ONLY' and anchors printed on each sheet. It was like the old Izal toilet paper. The list goes on, and on!

Big D.

Captain David Pentreath D.S.O. He was in his late forties to early fifties at the time. That was quite old compared to me and the rest of us. He's my old man's age and commanded a lot of respect. Respect he'd earned with his career of thirty years in the mob already and had four gold rings on his sleeves. He was a Fleet Air Arm trained pilot who flew Phantoms and other aircraft. He'd commanded other warships and was a jolly good chee-ap! Of good breeding and stiff upper lip.

He was and still is more like Roger Moore than Roger Moore is! Frightfully posh, with shiny, Brylcreamed brown hair, 6' tall and square jawed... better looking than old Rog! I used to have to wake him up from his limited sleep with the more important messages that demanded his attention. It was a bit of a chore to have to shake him. I'd tell his steward, if he was there, that I was going to have to wake him. I didn't like doing it for fear of him saying 'I've only been asleep for five minutes and you wake me to tell me THIS?' He never did of course, I had to creep in and give him a gentle shake in his wooden panelled little cabin. He'd always wake easily and make a snap decision there and then. Or he'd get up if he needed to, and he would deal with whatever it was that required his attention. He had one hell of a responsibility. He always addressed his ships company over the Tannoy every day and gave his message of the day. Not like bosses of large organisations today who you only get to see once in a blue moon and they haven't got a clue what you do for a living. Big D, I'm pretty sure knew just about everyone's name onboard. He certainly remembered mine at a re-union twenty odd years later. A true gent.

He's still going strong, happily retired and keeps himself busy on his yacht, sailing around the Needles off the Isle of Wight.

He had a team of officers, a commander, whose name escapes me. It was only as I was leaving the ship I had a conversation with the Commander and it turned out he was born in my village!

A 1st Lieutenant (aka; the 'Jimmy', Iain Henderson), a man who, in my opinion and I may be wrong, was born with a silver spoon in his cakehole. Turns out he's a nice chap but I didn't like him at the time. He was a small, (sorry about this) weasel-like man in his mid-twenties I guess, who was career minded and seemed ruthless. A Fleet Air Arm Buccaneer Pilot, he was to me rather like the young Caesar in The Life of Brian. 'Fwing him to the floor Centoowian!' Although he didn't have a speech impediment, his vocal skills were excellent, if a little nasal. I'm picking... He always seemed very fresh faced almost 'skin'. (Skin was a term we used for someone fresh faced or who didn't need to shave every day, as opposed to 'Scurrs' that meant rough and unshaven looking.

Years and years later, at the time when HMS Plymouth was closing down at the end of her career as a museum, Big D and Hendo turned up to say a few emotional words. I sneaked out of proceedings because I'd got a bone to pick with Hendo…

One day at sea, I was with Stevie Mac painting the bridge roof. There was a strip of wooden beading around the edge of the bridge roof, like a gutter but just decorative as far as I could tell. The beading needed painting too but there wasn't any beige left in the paint store. We were at sea and there was nowhere to get any more paint from! Hendo came up to inspect our handiwork. There we were in our paint spattered ovies (overalls, everything has a nickname) and he said "what about the beading paint Riley?" I said "we've run out", "well FIND some Riley!" I said "there isn't any Sir!" Then he said..."well MAKE SOME RILEY!" I couldn't believe it! The thought of DQ's (Detention Quarters - RN prison) put me off snotting him and I'm not a fighting man as you know! I was fuming at the time.

So, off I scuttled from the proceedings and I went in search of a can of paint. I found a bloke working on the upper deck and he was painting too! I asked him for the oldest, paint dribbled and dented, ancient tin of paint that he had and could spare for a blag. He came back with just the ticket... it even had a dried up brush stuck solid to the lid. I went back down to the hangar where his speech was just coming to an end and I approached. I stood next to him with the tin and leant over the microphone, I said, "Sir? Do you remember asking for that beading paint all those years ago? It has taken me a while, but here it is!" He beamed a huge smile and laughed, the audience caught the gist pretty quickly and gave a round of applause for that and his speech. He walked around the ship for the rest of the day holding his tin of paint. He didn't go and sort the beading out though! I hope he's still got it on his mantelpiece...

Under the Jimmy were all of the other officers, some great blokes, others not so great! Sid's arch enemy for one, who was particularly mean in his approach to managing men, I won't give him a mench...

Under the command of Big D we, after all of the trials, were pretty tight and would be ready to go to war, if ever invited to one. (Yeah RIGHT!). I have to say now though, that I take my hat off to young lads & lasses who join the military nowadays, because they can pretty safely (or unsafely) say, that they're going to get shot at! So, to join up knowing that there are very real risks involved, and they still volunteer, well, they are indeed very brave. Everyone takes a risk just going to work, commuting even, but they have the muck and bullets risk on top of that.

Under all of the officers were the Fleet Chiefs. There was one who was the Regulator, a man to be feared... best to avoid him. There were the Chief Petty Officers and the Petty Officers, who all had their own mess decks. Then there were Leading hands, usually a couple to each mess, they were directly in charge of us, similar in rank to a corporal and we called them 'Hookies', or individually 'Hooky'. They were also known as 'Killicks'. Then it was AB's, with one star, that meant you were 'able'. Then lowest of the low, the junior ranks (Sprogs). We had Hutch, (Roddy Hutcheson), as one of our Killick Buntings, whose first impression I explained earlier. He was a hard drinking, beefy bloke with hundreds of sea stories, who'd have you hooked waiting for his punch lines. He has a tattoo on his back of Jesus at the tiller of a tall ship with waves coming over the deck. It must have been what it was like when he joined. He had a drunk of a mate in the Seaman's mess called Mickey Divine, who on one occasion was very interested in Knotty's prized bottle of Old Spice aftershave. Knotty handed it to him, he sniffed it and went to put a drop in the palm of his hand. Then it went straight up to his lips like a hip flask! Knotty managed to grab it off him, but he'd drunk about half of it! He was a right one, a mess really, a shipwreck of a bloke, he couldn't have been much over twenty five but he looked much older! His hair was thinning on top and he had a couple of teeth missing. Mickey gave us a demonstration once of how you sieve Brasso metal polish through a slice of bread, into a glass and drink that! He also allegedly had a penchant for ME7, the floor polish we used to use on the deck! He'd hold the plastic one gallon bottle like a cider flagon, no wonder he always looked ill! Last I heard of him, his parents had locked him in his bedroom to dry him out, but he climbed out of his window and slid down the drainpipe faster than he intended and broke some bones.

We had Alistair 'Sweeny' Todd, who was our other Killick Bunting, a complete nutcase and a very funny bloke, he'd have been in his mid-twenties perhaps. Mad as a fish, but a manic depressive, hated being at sea and I haven't seen him since nineteen eighty two.

The others in the mess I'll try to recall, I'll start at A.

A. Knotty; Richard Ash, further to tho initial meeting at Pembroke. Then, he was very fashionable, a New Romantic styled, hairy, little dark skinned bloke, of unknown origin. I thought probably Turkish but he wasn't. Since the purple sheets days we became best of mates and had many good times, usually revolving around drinking, we still do for that matter. He is as I'm writing, assisting with editing and jogging my memory, so thanks for that mate! (Even though you did get us beaten up in Dumf's).

Catchphrase: "I'm wiv me mates, me real mates". (A phrase still referred to today, on a regular basis, referring to a time when he went out with the elders of the mess who got him absolutely slaughtered on scrumpy. He's got lots of mates).

Alistair 'Sweeny' Todd, as mentioned above, was a very funny bloke who did pigeon impressions too.

Catchphrase; "oooh oooh oooh" and (said quickly) "Tommy Doak, Tommy Doak, Tommy-Tommy Doak, oooh!" (you had to be there perhaps...).

B. Mal Banfield; the perv, with a flat nose and silver rimmed glasses, who had interesting pictures of his girlfriend that he kept very closely guarded.

Catchphrase; "phwoor!"

C. Col Riley; a flat-capped Yorkshireman, older than his years and a fucking nice bloke.

Catchphrase; "heyoop ladd?"

Andy 'Chalky' Selby; He is of mixed race, Afro Caribbean and white. Now racist as it sounds these days, things just weren't the same then. In my heart he's Chalky, he's one of my very best mates, but you can't shout 'HEY! CHALKY' across a bar now, so it's "Andy! You're round!" His nickname is endearIng but times have changed and absolutely no malice was ever meant.

Catchphrases; "wasn't me mate", and "oh God you won't belieeeeeve what just happened".

D. Dom Goldsack; a certain Cornish Fisherman, a huge bloke who'd just pick you up and walk you out of a pub under his arm if you were in any bother. He'd hammer fist your assailant on the top of his head at the same time, dropping him instantly!

Catchphrase; "AHA HA HA!"

Tommy Doak; our boss, a Chief Yeoman (Signals). He'd got a few years in and was very experienced. Seemed old to me back then, only because I was so young! There doesn't seem so much of an age gap now. Odd that one, isn't it? A great sense of humour... although always seemed so serious at the time.

Catchphrase; "mah boys!"

E. Enoch! Now y'know what I said before, well this still applies, Tony 'Enoch' Powell, he was so dark skinned that you couldn't see his numerous tattoos, he loved his little 'natty dreads', he was a big dude. We went to his wedding in 1980, in Birmingham. It had been snowing like mad. I'd got one suit, a three piece, light blue striped number, with huge lapels and flares. I remember going arse over tit on a slushy pavement and, had to walk around with a soggy arse for the first hour. He'd invited us lot along to his reception do. The guests being a majority of Afro Caribbean people, (most of us had never really met any Black people before apart from Enoch & Chalky. There weren't any Asians onboard either. I'd only met two or three Asians at that time, one (the only one) at school and a couple at the factory where I did my apprenticeship (Dank's of Netherton). The Asian bloke that I remember from Dank's could hardly speak any English and used to walk around the shop floor saying either "plenty painty painty" or "plenty sweepy sweepy" obviously dependant on his task at the time.

Back to the wedding in the snow, I do that, digress that is. I do it after a couple of pints mostly, go completely off on a tangent and then I can't remember where the fuck I was. It helps if there's someone with you who is listening. Obviously writing is easier, because you only have to look back a paragraph and get back to it. Billy Connolly is a master at it, he's in a league of his own. I've done it again haven't I?

It was a little worrying at first but after a few wee swallies we all had a great time!

Getting back to the ship was a big problem that weekend. The snow got worse and we had to set off to get the train back to Scotland. Stevie Windle, Foggie, Mac McClain and Knotty stayed at my mum & dad's. But the Sunday morning when we had to go to get a train back to Scotland, the snow was so deep the cars on the drive were just smooth mounds of snow. The only car that we could get up the road was my Brother David's VW beetle and he ferried us all up to Wolverhampton station, I think we were the only car on the road.

He calls himself 'Cozy Powell' now. I don't think he's ever been called Baden. I think he'd frighten the kids anyway.

Catchphrase; yawning, he yawned and slept a lot.

F. Alan 'Foggy' Fothergill; he had the best fringe except maybe for Stevie Windle...

very cool, liked his tatts, slightly goofy teeth with a gap between his front ones and bulging eyes. He had a specially grown long little finger nail specifically for the purpose of nose picking. He would stare at you and say "what you on abaat you? Eh?" My best Telfordish accent in print there.

One wind-up with Foggy was where Knotty suggested to him that he went to the Navigating Officers cabin to request the keys to the Pool Room. He was slightly suspicious but fell for it. Anyway once it was explained to him that the pool table had highly sensitive springs on each of the four corners to keep the table completely static in swelling seas and therefore the balls wouldn't roll about. Sure enough he bit and went to ask the N.O. for the keys…

Catchphrase; as above.

Colin 'Fez' Parker; he was a late joiner, probably in early eighty two, he had the unenviable task of having the bottom bunk right underneath Hutch. Particularly unenviable when Hutch one night was asleep in the 'coma position', which I have to say is a very good position to sleep in with a belly full of booze. Fez had his head hanging out a little, fast asleep, and Hutch also fast asleep, stirred... MMMMP?

(The sound of someone about to blow chunks) MMMMMMMMMP?? Poor Fez got the lot!

Catchphrase: "aaw fuh fuck sake man!"

G. No G's

H. Roddy 'Hutch' Hutcheson, the Killick of the mess, slept in the middle bunk nearest the mess square, so he could keep an eye on us probably. Also being a large unit, the middle bunk was easier for him to swing into. It was his mess and he was the biggest, so he could sleep where he wanted to quite frankly. He kept me in check because I was a bit mouthy on occasion, like informing him once (not my best decision) to announce, with an audience, to him, his new nickname and what we all called him behind his back - 'FUB' (Fat Ugly Bastard). Let's just say, it didn't go down too well. Me and Hutch didn't see eye to eye in those days, he probably (no definitely) thought I was a cheeky wee shite and I thought he was unreasonable. I'm glad to say that we're good mates now. (The years have been kind... ish).

Catch Phrase; "what the fuck ya deeein?"

'H' I think he was called was an older bloke, I can't remember his name but I think he retired or something before we went down South, he must've joined when Nelson was a boy. I remember he was a big old bloke (probably only in his 30's) he had an incredible comb over where one side of his hair was really long. Kind of an un-trendy version of Phil Oakey's from The Human League. Well not exactly like his because H had none on top! He used to comb it carefully and accurately all over the whole top of his head. Including the crown and pat it into place, it was as thick as a horse's tail! It covered his bald scalp perfectly... until that is, when he went out on the upper deck, where this big flap of hair would be set free to flow over his shoulder in the wind, like a big floppy eared dog with its head out of the car window. He'd struggle to keep it in place, a really funny sight. Then once back inside, the comb would come out and order would be restored.

Catchphrase; I actually can't remember a word he ever said! (Sorry!).

I. Ian 'Dig Dig' Brown; dunno what happened to him. He was a huge musclebound body builder with fine, brown, middle parted hair. Spent most of his spare time honing his body in a lifelong struggle to get rid of an overlying layer of fat that disguised his muscle very well. He was determined to enter the Field Gun team. He had previously done a stint on the R.N. Display Team, he was very proud of that. We used to call it the R.N. Ballet Team which would really piss him off! They used to do exercises on a suspended acrobat type display and jump over wooden horses, wearing tights and vests. No wonder he wanted to improve his image by getting on the Field Gun.

Catchphrase; "DIG DIG!"

J. Nope.

K. No

L. No

M. Mac McCleod; a tough wee Scotsman, who insisted on whacking his dick on the chain around the hatch and the handles on the ladder. He always wore a big fringe under his beret, he was really ROMFT, (Roll On My Fucking Time) and due to leave the Navy but he was kept in for the Falklands, he was not a happy bunny.

Catchphrase; "get tae fuck, ya wee shite ye!"

N. vacant

O. N/A

P. 'Doc' Peddy; funny how you just don't know some people's first names, Doc was The Doc, or Medic onboard. He was (seemed) ancient, three good conduct stripes on his arm, would stitch you up in his sick bay and administer black bombers for when you were constipated or the equivalent opposite medication for when you weren't. He had a bushy beard, baldy head, smoked roll-ups and was exactly the same shape as the hole in hatch. What I mean by that is that a hatch going down into a mess or compartment below, would be clipped down to be water tight in certain situations. It would have a smaller oval hatch in the middle of the main hatch, which you could open and drop through. The Doc somehow used to squeeze through there with relative ease! He used to put his belt on with a boomerang!

Catchphrase; "one o' these three times a dee".

Q. ...

R. Riley; I'll put me in here, 'Spike', Catchphrase "wo'ne urt!"

Alan (Scotty) Ronald; he was in our mess by default. He had a run in with someone in his mess, the seaman's mess next door, so they put him in with us and what a very good idea that was, and he must've planned it all along. (Typical stormy Jock).

Catchphrase; "It wasnae me!"

S. Stevie 'Mac' McGarry; the Scouser of the mess, an incredibly dedicated fitness fanatic, still is! A couple of years older than me, we met on the train going down to Plymouth on the way to HMS Raleigh on 4th December 1979. I remember getting on the train, I had a suitcase and I'd filled it as per the instructions I was given. With stuff like pyjamas, pants, socks, washing kit, civvies etc. I hadn't worn any PJ's (or as they were known; Brown Hatters Overalls) since I was a kid, so I was worried that they might actually make me wear them!

I was waved off by my Dad at Wolverhampton station, looked in my bag... well y'know, I thought there may have been a good luck message, or at least a bacon sandwich... bugger all! I'm not sure but I could swear I saw him actually running back to the car, I think that was the day they moved house.

Anyway, I wandered down the train, one of the old fashioned ones they still had on the network then. The ones with wooden cabins and those springy seats that were always too bloody hot The heat came from under the seats and slow roasted your undercarriage. I wandered down to the buffet car where I met Steve, drinking Newkie Brown, with John Reed, and some others, I'm not sure if Duncan 'Scouse' Spence, from Newcastle oddly, and Kev 'Geordie' Watson, also from Newcastle, oddly, were there too. So we had a few 'Broons' and discussed how worried we were about joining the Navy and wearing brown hatter's overalls. I think in truth we were shitting ourselves!

Steve I think did get to Field Gun, (Google it!)

He'd do press-ups with thirty kilos on his back, a tough little bugger who loves a Guinness or three. With jet black side parted hair and a square blue stubble jaw, stocky and always smiling. We went all the way through Raleigh and Mercury and then joined the Plymouth together. Still great mates.

Catchphrase; "der, der, I'll 'av a Guinness".

SID! Andrew 'Sid' Henry; the loveable rogue who was into The Sex Pistols (hence 'Sid' Vicious), Siouxsie and the Banshees', lots of unheard of punk bands (Peter and the Test Tube Babies, being one of them) and was the one who had the best boogie box, the chosen technology at the time, for listening to music on the move. He certainly widened my eyes to music. He managed to grow a short Mohican and get a little colour on the tips, but was advised to get rid, (told in no uncertain terms more like) much to his disdain. A certain officer made his life a misery... who, at one point, sent him to the Royal Naval Hospital Haslar, to go on a course to lose weight! Unbelievable, even then! It didn't make a lot of difference to Sid, a Londoner, who was developing a keen interest for tattoos. Sid was / is always a laugh and would without hesitation, grow a Mohican right now, if only he could!

Catchphrase; "nah mate... fack it!"

T. 'Taff' the Reggie, he was in my gulch, I'm sure he was posted to live in the RO's mess to keep an eye on us lot! He was a broad Welshman in accent and chest diameter, with a fine beard.

Catchphrase: "Reg office! NOW!"

Alistair 'Sweeny' Todd, already done.

David 'Tug' Wilson; a shy, slightly goofy toothed lad who at the time lacked a bit of confidence but a nice bloke, even skinnier than me! (Then...).

U. ( )

V. ?

W. Darren 'Spider' Webb; an absolute nutter, with a face to match, always grinning, pale skinned with ginger curly hair. He had freckles and a little pot belly that he seemed to love and nurture. Last time I saw him he'd obviously been nurturing it to the extreme. He was a broad Yorkshireman and liked a reet good laugh. He'd always tell stories about his antics which usually ended up with him running away and he'd do a Billy Wizz impression.

Catchphrase; "I were like, waaaaah!'

'Wee Stevie' Windle; frae Kirkcaldy, the owner of the best fringe at the time; not the owner of a fringe at all now, I must say. Where the fuck did you go (went off radar years ago) Steve? He was a one for the ladies, never had a problem 'trapping', nothing to do with beavers, although...

Anyway he was most certainly one of the 'in crowd'.

Catchphrase; "are we away fer a wee swalley?"

Shiner Wright. Chief Radio Supervisor; big, broad shouldered and accented Scotsman, who for all I knew spent most of his time in the MCO.

Catchphrase; "Spike... Ah like Spike!"

There were of course many other characters on the ship, many whose names come up as 'oh yeah, remember him?...'kin 'ell!' And I really am useless with names, I'm amazed I've remembered THAT LOT!

John Fearon THE Stoker of all Stokers, 'Roughie', 'Jan' Joplin, 'Donna' Summers, 'Gramps' Harsent, Bill Alderson, Bob Donkin, Bryn Hopper, Chris 'Jack' Warner. Jack, I will mention later but he was our hero! I can't remember who told me, a few years later but the buzz was that he'd committed suicide. Probably due to what they now call P.T.S.D. Which when I thought about what he must have gone through, was almost understandable. We used to travel from Edinburgh quite often on the train, he'd get off at Stoke, the stop before mine at Wolverhampton and so we'd have a few beers on the train together when we were off on leave or going back up North. Very sad…

Davy Norman; never short of a joke or eight.

Gaz Borthwick; a wannabe RO and he knows it!

'Mad Mac' McGhie, the clue's in the name, rarely seen without his WWI faded brown leather fighter pilots elmet and goggles, oh and his snakeskin cowboy boots!

John 'H' 'Harry' Harrison.

Kevan Watton (still fucking in! Although in the army in Norway).

Roger 'Titch' Middleton (mucho respecto!),

Sean Roche, Stef Olszok, Steve 'Howie' Howard, Alan Golightly, Colin Sievwright, Dave 'Billy The' Kidd.

Buster Brown the PO Seaman, I always got on with him, everyone did. He had a face only a mother could love, he was inflicted by some sort of skin disorder but he didn't give a fuck, he was a right laugh. I spotted him some years later in Fuengirola, Spain, I saw him from Gibraltar, he was so easily recognisable, I tried to shout him but he was too far away! (Only joking) we had a few beers and a catch up. I was living in Spain at the time. Neither of us could have known it but I found out a few years later when I spoke to him at a reunion, the day we said 'bye' to each other and he walked around the corner, I went back to work, he looked the wrong way to cross the road and got run over, breaking almost every bone in his body! Talk about a survivor!

Dave Laird, Frank Galloway, Geoff Abbott, Jimmy Riddock, John Bain, John Blackwell, John Speed, John 'Jan' Waterfield, Kev Jackson, John McDermott, Mark Robinson, Mervyn Nash, Phil Hodgson, Phil 'Plum' Lumsden, Phil Coombs, Ray Potts, Robert Bagwell, Robert Mcilvenny, Steve Bladen, Bryn Hopper, George Crully.

George was an incredibly stocky, muscular lad, I remember shaving his head once, to a crew cut, which weren't allowed then. Apparently if you had a grade one and you fell in the oggin (the sea), no-one would be able to pull you out by your hair! That meant that you'd drown, obviously. Bizarre! Anyway I shaved his head, I had to shave around a huge raised mole he had on his crown, I never could get to those last few hairs and so he'd walk around with a bit of an antennae just to highlight his mole.

There were more and to those I've missed

Well, you are, missed that is!

Jack (Jolly Jack that is, likes a 'mench'!).

Slog (the daily grind).

A typical day onboard could be a bit of a slog at times. Being young, of course you don't really want to be cooped up on / in a metal tub four hundred and fifty feet by about twenty (a very rough guesstimate). By the way, I'm not writing a factual reference book here, but well, it's bigger than a prison cell, I know where I'd rather be... give me a prison cell any day!

The 'call to hands' a boson's call, would come over the Tannoy at 7am, you'd roll out of your scratcher (pit, bunk or bed), zip it up, grab your wash bag and don a towel, go up the ladder, avoiding any mop handles that would inevitably be shoved up your towel to get you up the ladder and through the hatch quicker. You go through the toilet & shower routine. Once dressed, a fag before breakfast on your pit and you'd make your way down to the galley. Full English was on display every day, unless eggs had run out, but we were rarely at sea for more than five nights in a row.

We shared the queue for the galley with the Dhobi Wallahs, the Chinese Laundrymen. They used to live in a compartment at the stern, where they'd sleep on their ironing boards in really cramped conditions. They would do all of your laundry, for a price, and give it back to you in a compressed cube of steam ironed items, tied up with brown string. You didn't want to get in debt with them, they didn't speak much English but they knew about money! Catchphrase; "you pay for flucky dhoby, you flucky pay now, or big twubble!" They'd queue for scran with us, I'm pretty sure we had crockery plates on that ship because I remember doing pot wash for a while, ooh that's another story... Anyway whatever we had, plates or compartmentalised stainless steel trays, the Chogi's (we called them, please don't tell me THAT's racist now too!) had a large bowl (a Chogi Nosh bowl) that everything in order from the display would go in. Salted porridge ("why put salt in?", "Because it's a Scottish ship with a majority of Scots onboard and Scots eat porridge with FUCKING SALT IN, ALRIGHT?" "Ok, jeez! I was only asking..."

So, porridge, scrambled egg, bacon, sausage... Other meal times, they'd pile in stew, a chop, veg, gravy, pudding AND custard, all in the one Chogi Nosh bowl! They'd sit down, holding the bowl in one hand and shovel in the lot, using chopsticks, into their eager mouths, (like Shite Hawk chicks) with a bowl-to-face distance of about two inches. I think they ate as a necessity rather than anything else. Sorry...'Shite Hawk' = Seagull.

Eating had to be done reasonably quickly, so that everyone could get through the process and you'd want to lie on your pit with another fag and a cup of tea, before starting work at eight am. Then you'd be given tasks to do, either manning the bridge, signal deck, MCO, or cleaning or painting something. Twenty four hour duties would be interwoven into a working day so you could be on duty after midday or lunch for the afternoon and you'd get a couple of hours off, time to eat and then do one of the 'dog' watches (shifts). The shifts seemed to go on and on, a never ending-grind, especially on defence watches; six on, six off, you'd quite quickly forget what day it was!

My usual workstation was on the bridge, usually with either Hutch or Sweeney. I'd have to scrub and mop the deck during the morning watch before the Skipper came up for a view. Most people avoided ever walking on someone's wet deck that they'd just scrubbed unless it was unavoidable, in which case you wouldn't mind too much, well you would if you'd just polished the bastard and it was still wet. Some 'Ruperts' (pompous officers) would just walk all over it without a thought for you on your hands and knees, scrubbing away like Hilda Ogden. Some like to show their superiority in odd ways...

Big D would usually make an appearance at about 06:30, I'd be scrubbing the blobby rubber deck tiles, just before the end of my watch and he'd always say "morning Riley, what's going on then?" "Well Sir, I've just got this section to do..." (How should I fucking know I've been on my hands and knees for the last hour?) He wouldn't deliberately walk on the wet bits though.

The rest of your shift would be keeping the bridge log of signals that are passed backwards and forwards. Relaying messages to the OOW or the Skipper that came from other ships via the radios, flags, flashing light or paper messages from the MCO. Quieter periods of time when you weren't on duty covering the watch would be spent maintaining the lanterns, scrubbing, chipping and, or painting stuff. A certain amount of skiving had to be done or it would seem like you didn't get any free time at all. So our 'part of ship' (the part of the ship you were responsible for) as Buntings, was be the signal deck (where the signal lanterns and entrance to the mast is). No-one ever found us kipping in the mast. As I said earlier, there were sections inside with a ladder going up the middle, all the way up to the top. We sometimes had to go all the way up there and out of the hatch at the very top to paint the yard arms, a good sixty foot drop to the deck! I remember the first time I had to do that, I got a safety harness from the paint store and went up there. When I opened the hatch at the top and ventured out, it was really scary. As the ship rolled with the wave motion, you can imagine how much the movement is when it's transferred to the top of the mast! First you fasten the clip to something solid, then you had to climb out onto the yardarm, clinging like a chameleon to the steel tubing, with legs like a schoolgirls plait at your other end wrapped around the yardarm. Once in that position, a tin of paint and a brush had to be handed to you. That meant letting go with one hand. I ended up painting with my nose, perched on the edge of the tin and making brush strokes with one hand about an inch beyond the tin. Then I'd slide forward another inch to do the next bit. Unclipping to get over a strut was even more un-nerving!

Intermingled with everything that we all (Sprogs, (RO2's)) had to complete were our Task Books, for the next step up the ladder, career wise. We all managed to get our * on our badges making us RO1's, the same as an AB, similar to a Lance Corporal, by the end of '81. I don't think it was particularly difficult but seemed a chore to have to complete at the time.

I remember one afternoon, me and Sid and Knotty bought a pie each and a can of 'goffer' and went up into the third section of the mast, two floors up actually inside the mast. We filled it with flag bags to get comfortable, had a little feast and a sleep. It was pitch dark in there, you couldn't see your pie in front of your nose, but you could see down below and the bottom section was lit. So if anyone was stood down there looking up, you could see them, but they couldn't see you, it would just be blackness above. We were suddenly woken from sleep by the sound of the metal clips being undone on the door, I looked down as a shaft of light came into the bottom section and Mal Banfield's bespectacled face strained to look upwards. He switched the light on down there and shut the door. He was squinting, straining to see up into the darkness. He obviously couldn't see anything, least of all US - looking down at him! Hands over our mouths, he shut the door and he actually started climbing the ladder, he got to the second section. He was just below us, he looked up, he still couldn't see us looking down, and he was just a couple of feet away. We thought he was looking for Sid as he'd been missing for a couple of hours. Then as he was stood there he started undoing his trousers, pulled them down half way and sat on a flag bag. Well we were bursting to laugh, I don't know how we kept it in. He was about to have a wank! I couldn't believe it. I picked up something metal and scraped it on the bulkhead, Mal froze... looking all around with his hands over his bits, I whispered whoooooooooh!" as Sid said spookily "Maaaal". He pulled his trousers up and shot down the ladder and out of the door like a scalded cat! Fucking hell, we fell about laughing.

Well, we just had to go down the mess as he'd obviously seek sanctuary down there. So we made our way down to the mess, and there he was, sat looking as white as a sheet. He was saying "the fucking mast's haunted, honest!" "What do you mean?" "I just went up there to get something, (yeah right) there was no-one else in there and I heard a creepy noise, I shit myself!" In unison we repeated… "whoooooooooh Maaaal" and started laughing, he said "YOU FUCKIN' BASTARDS!!" "Yeah Mal, you won't be going up there for a wank again will you?" Then he told us that he'd once found a sailor hanging by his neck inside the mast on his last ship! Awkward…

Another job that we had to take turns at was 'Spud Bosun' or 'Pot Wash' where we'd come away from normal duties and help out in the galley preparing veg, making up the tea and coffee urns, topping up the juice machines and washing all the crockery and cutlery. The spud peeling and chopping them up into chips and boiled potato shapes was the most laborious task. You wouldn't be working through the night but you had to do all of the prep the night before, after tea. You'd have to fill three square twenty two gallon tubs with spuds and chips. There was a water powered little peeler thing that you'd chuck spuds or carrots in to peel them by giving them a go at an abrasive wall of death. It was a good laugh, you'd get to walk around in your ovies all day. I even designed an arm badge to replace my crossed flags with a potato and a couple of crossed knives. I remember once, I was Spud Bosun when we did a visit to Newcastle in '81, we came in under the bridges up the river right into the town (toon). I was desperate to go out with the lads for a run ashore and managed to persuade the PO Chef to let me do the spuds early. So I did them during the afternoon, before and just after tea, and managed to get ashore with the others on time. Usual routine, chuck your trendy stuff onto the quayside, pick it up on the way into town and off we'd go. We went drinking around the Metro Centre, I think it was called. I pulled some bird in a nightclub, who looked like Suzy Quattro... she probably didn't in reality, and she was a little rough around the edges. She suggested we go back to hers, she probably didn't have the taxi fare, so off we went, and it was bloody miles!

We drove into the middle of a huge and really rough looking housing estate. Council houses with boarded up windows and rubbish all over the place. The driver pulled up outside a semi-detached house with boarded up front windows, I paid the driver and asked him to come back at six and he promised that he would.

We got out and went up to the house, looking through a missing plank on the front window she shouted at a bloke who was lying on the settee, who let us in. He was her cousin or something, he showed me his new tattoo... 'ELVIS', inked on the inside edge of one of his fingers, all red and probably infected, "nice mate". He left... leaving us there alone, well, not quite.

There was no carpet just some floorboards, I say some because, some were where the window should be and others were crackling in the fireplace! There was damp washing everywhere. She said that we'd have to sleep on the sofa bed that she started pulling out, under the front window. We couldn't go upstairs because the baby was sleeping up there and someone had broken in and tricd to steal her hot water tank. They couldn't get it out, so they stabbed holes in it and soaked the bed! Oh my fucking God, what the hell am I doing here? I didn't sleep a wink. I did do the necessary… well, I was there wasn't I? It'd be rude not to. I stayed awake all night though, I felt sorry for her really. The sun started to come through the missing floorboard gap and I could see she'd got dirty fingernails. I kept looking outside and as good as gold at six, the taxi turned up. A kiss on the cheek and I was out of there! I think the driver was worried about me and he took me back to the ship, asking me lots of questions. I got back in time to get the tea and coffee ready for breakfast, and I didn't have to go see the Doc! Bonus!

The Russian Submarine Incident.

Being based in Rosyth was a bit of a bind really because it was a very long way from home! Seventy five percent of the ships company was Scottish so it wasn't so bad for them, unless you were Mad Mac who lived so far North the whole winter was dark! We'd get the train from Inverkeithing and go over the big red Forth Rail Bridge to Edinburgh and then I'd get a train straight through to Wolverhampton. We'd usually get off early on a Friday, and so I used to get home in time to go out for a drink with my brother Dave. Paul, my youngest brother, was too young then. On the approach to one weekend we were on short notice for going to sea to follow Russian Subs and those Russian fishing boats that had more antennae than a crowd of cockroaches, 'you're not fishing... are you Boris?' Anyway we had to make a special application for leave and if you lived any more than six hours away you weren't going to be allowed to go. But I'd arranged to meet a girl who I'd met on holiday at a Warners campsite on the Isle of Wight, me and Knotty went there for a summer holiday, he pulled a Red Coat! He even got engaged to her… for a few days! (No ring involved). I got the burger-flipper! She was coming up on the train to my Mum and Dads from the Isle of Wight and I was coming down from Scotland to see her for the weekend.

Well, home was six hours away if you were on The Silver Bullet! I managed to get my leave anyway, so off I fucked! Dad picked me up from the station and she was there when I got home. Brilliant! We were sat in the pub, The Cross in Kingswinford and Mum appeared, in the pub. She said "Simon, they want you to go back!" I couldn't believe it! I apparently went as white as a sheet! I'd never get back in time and this girl had come all the way up here to see me! We called the train station and the coach companies but there wasn't another train till later on and I would never get back in time. I spoke to Taff on the phone, who obviously couldn't get to Wales and he said that it'd be alright as long as I got there before two in the morning. There was no choice, I had to leave my burger flipper there for Dave to take to the station in his VW Beetle. While me, Mum and Dad took it in turns driving Mum's yellow Vauxhall Cavalier 1.6L, all the way up to Rosyth! It took us about six hours but we'd made it before two am! I was in the clear, problem was, that the ship had already buggered off! Mum and Dad started off on the long journey back home whilst I was shown to an accommodation block in HMS Cochrane the shore base adjacent to Rosyth Naval Base. The following morning, there were quite a few of us that hadn't made it and we were all in the shit for sure. There were about sixty of us in total, some of the early arrivals had been flown out by helicopter the rest of us were split in to two groups. Half the group were sent home on rail warrants after a couple of days hanging around in the NAAFI waiting for the bar to open. The rest of us were sent off to a ski resort called Aviemore. The only problem was that it was autumn. There was no snow... not a ski in sight. We spent a couple of days hiking, orienteering and camping, it was quite nice really, a bit of a skive actually. We were driven there and back in a blue flatbed seven and a half tonner with a blue canopy over the back, which said R.N. in white on the side. It wasn't the most comfortable journey. When we got back the 'Old Girl' was back tied-up alongside in Rosyth again. We all went back onboard and we were informed that we were indeed, 'in the shit'...

I was told that I had got 'The Captain's Table', along with everyone else, it was like going to court, you had to turn up in No1's, immaculate. Shoes shined, creases all in the right places and cap in hand. I waited outside the Captain's cabin, feeling really nervous. The door opened, I was called (bawled) in. I stepped inside, put my cap on, saluted then took it off again in one movement with my right hand gripping the left rim whipping it off and held it under my arm on my right side. The fringe could present a problem at a time like this, you'd have to try and blow upwards if it flopped, with your bottom lip protruding and hope that the air pressure released would lift it into a manageable position without flicking your head about to move it. The Master at Arms was there, my boss Tommy Doak and so was Taff. It was all very serious. I presented my case by saying that I'd got back within the time that Taff had told me on the phone.

Luckily Taff didn't dispute it, he corroborated my story and I was excused.

Out of the forty of us it was only me that got away with it.

It turned out that everyone else got punishment that meant No 9's (extra duties doing some shit jobs) and a fine of £25.00!

Knotty was one of the ones who didn't make it back he'd only gone to see a girl in Kirkcaldy for fuck sake, about twenty miles away, but he just didn't come back! I didn't see the girl from the Isle of Wight again!

Everyone onboard would have traded places with us, even done the No 9's as they'd spent a few days in Harry roughers, around the Hebrides, chasing the Russian warship Kiev around and had a shit time of it! They went so far north they got their 'Blue Nose certificates' for sailing above a certain latitude in Harry icer's.

Windies Deployment.

The time was passing and we were approaching our promised six month deployment to the West Indies, we were all fired up for it and raring to go. We'd spent eighteen months getting the ship ready for anything. We visited places like Breast, Malmo, St Peter Port and London, where we went under the Tower Bridge and tied up alongside HMS Belfast. So we were really ready for a proper trip, seeing the world as it were / was / is? The plan was to go to Gibraltar for a weekend leave, take part in Operation Springtrain for a few days, then two or three weeks tarting the ship up. Then at last sail to Florida and Miami. We were to be the West Indies Guard Ship for a couple of months. I'd actually be able to experience for myself all of the stories that the 'old salts' had told us about these places. Banyan's (BBQ's) on the beach, exotic ladies, exotic drinking, exotic tropical weather and exotic diseases, the lot!

We all got a couple of weeks leave in turns, the ship was running on half Ships Company for a few weeks alongside in Rosyth. Once that was done, we actually set off for the Med. It was the end of March nineteen eighty two.

Operation Springtrain was our last job before we were actually ready to go off to paradise. Springtrain was a mock war that we'd take part in with the Yanks and other ships from NATO countries, we set sail for Gibraltar. It was really exciting, I remember the sea turning blue, rather than the usual grey or green that we were used to and the weather getting warmer. The sky got bigger as the clouds got smaller. We spent any time off sunning ourselves on the upper deck. Sometimes in front of the 4.5's and when there was a swell and we were heading into the wind, we'd get showered by fine spray to cool us down. It started to get really hot as we got to the other side of the Bay of Biscay.

After one afternoon spent 'bronzying' on the upper deck, we went back down the mess to clean up for rounds and Enoch began to complain that his skin was burning. Enoch, who had earlier been telling us about his Afro Caribbean heritage and the benefits of coconut oil, began to come up with huge tattooed blisters! I've never seen anything like it on a black man, or a white one for that matter. He'd got third degree burns! I felt sorry for him but it was hilarious. You know when someone hurts themselves, but it's funny too? You just can't help yourself! My younger brothers hate me for that! (I'm thinking; a Raleigh Chopper two up, down a dirt path, Dave & Paul. Paul facing backwards holding the back rest on the double seat. Dave lost control after the front wheel hit a pebble and Dave went veering off to the right at the side of a field (Paul followed, backwards). A luscious bed of fresh green stinging nettles were cunningly camouflaging a ditch and down they went, shorts and tee shirts offered little protection! Sorry but it still makes me laugh out loud now!).

We got to Gibraltar for a weekend run ashore, I followed the rest who knew the best places to go. The Hole In The Wall, a pub I remembered, but it's all a bit of a blur from then on if I'm honest, I don't remember much about it at all, I don't remember getting a lift back one night with MOD Plod in a Land Rover either!

We went to sea for Springtrain but doing military exercises with the Yanks has always been a risky business with their track record for FUBAR's & friendly fire incidents. One day in the Bay of Biscay I think it was, we were target practice for one of their heavily armed Gazelle helicopters. He was supposed to fire a live depth charge or something at a certain distance away from us to simulate an attack. Jeez! He must have dropped it about three feet away, it went off and the whole ship shook, I was in the mess when it went off with a hell of a bang and the reverberations made the side of the ship sound like it was flapping about violently. I think it was some sort of echo effect between the hull and the density of the water, but it was scary. Our mortars had a similar effect, there were three big mortar tubes on the quarter deck at the back of the ship, they were Anti-Submarine mortars and Christ they made a bang when they went off! They'd shoot off with a bang, the mortar would land in the water, the splash would die down, then… BOOM! The water would just erupt like a huge zit and then explode in a plume of white spray.

The four-fives too, they used to make a ridiculous bang, there were two barrels, obviously four point five inches, inside diameter. The shells themselves had a brass tip that was about the size of a small pointy hat, four point five inches across too. That was attached to the top of the three foot tall brass shell that had all the stuff that goes bang inside. That would project this massive bullet for miles and it would come sharp if it hit you! The OOW would give the warning that the gun was about to be fired, but when it did, it still made you jump out of your skin, no matter where you were on the ship. Of course my bunk was right underneath the bloody thing wasn't it? In the mess, everything would move when it fired. Secreted ashtrays would fall from their hiding places on the deck head pipes, things would fall over and it'd make you spill your tea. If you were on the bridge when it fired it was almost as if the air moved, you could feel the air pressure change, you could feel it in your guts, it almost hurt, I'm sure your feet would shift half an inch on the deck, I think everything moved half an inch. Then BANG! Another...BANG! BANG! BANG! BANG! There was a kind of a 'pinging' noise that would ring in my ears just after each bang. It was the sound the shell made when it landed on the deck, as it was spat out after releasing the pointy bit. Just like a massive revolver. I've still got that noise in my ears thirty two years later. When it's quiet it sounds like I'm sitting next to a refrigerator, or like the ringing in your ears after a rock concert, it just doesn't go away. Tinnitus has driven some to distraction, I can only hear it now because I've just been thinking about it.

The earphones I used to wear, when I was using the UHF radio didn't help, they cupped my ears and concentrated the sound coming from the speakers inside. They did the same job with the BANG from the four five's, by concentrating that too. I couldn't always stick my fingers in my ears because I'd be busy writing, so quite often I got the full volume in me lug 'oles. They worked in the exact opposite way to ear defenders, which most people were issued with on the upper deck. Still... you what??

This is our mess (3E), Hutch's bunk is in the middle there with the blue sleeping bag. A street sign is displayed, one I snaffled on the London trip. To the right between the iron and the ladder is the four five shell tube where my bunk was. Note the Betamax video, the buggery boards and a can of Irn Bru! If you're wondering what that thing above Hutch's pillow is, stuck to the buggery board. It's 'Tadger', Hutch's toy duck, who survived an attempted lynching after being kidnapped by Sid. Tadger went on to survive two tours of Afghanistan.

Bronzying on the upper scupper! Left to right Spider (holding it in), Dom, Scotty, Buster & Titch.

Harry Roughers! Photo; Al McIntyre.

Roughy on the 10 inch lantern, Steve McGarry and me on the port bridge wing.

1982 ships Co.

I'm bottom right. Photo; Al again.

2nd April 1982.

I can put some dates to everything from now on. Because as I said earlier, I had to record everything in the Bridge Log. I managed to grab hold of the log from Tommy Doak before he chucked it over the side, the best way of getting rid of confidential material. When we were on our way back to the U.K. I got hold of an alphabetically indexed note book and copied down the next one hundred and eight days. Then Tommy chucked the thing in the oggin. The log was actually called the Tactical Turnover Log and I copied it into my little diary on the 10th July 1982, I've still got it. In fact I'm looking at it now as I type. Inside the cover it says it's by me and then; *'it's not everything that happened but its most of it!'*

I won't say it's all completely factual and I won't get into any arguments with anyone who say's otherwise. It's probably not completely one hundred percent correct, as I didn't have all of the information to hand at the time. This is more a recording of my point of view and of how I recorded it at the time, misguided or not, it's what happened to me.

I'll copy what I wrote in the book verbatim, as I'm going and use that as a reference. I'll expand on everything I wrote as it comes to me, as I go through it. Some of the sentences will seem to be written badly but that's how I wrote them at the time, in note form. So here goes from Friday 2nd April 1982…

We were on our way to Gibraltar after the four days at sea on Operation Springtrain. My self and Knotty were prepared for our watch keeper's leave, we were both up on the bridge. It was early in the morning and light, our leave was to be spent on the beach on Gib, in Catalan Bay, with a few beers. This was to be followed by two to three more weeks there for an Assisted Maintenance Period, to get us ready for the deployment. We were going island hopping our way round the Windies and spending three weeks in Fort Lauderdale, where we would have a week's leave then we were going to work a day on / day off routine for the following two weeks, it was really happening, we'd worked so hard for it and achieved our goal. As we headed towards the Straits of Gibraltar, with Morocco to our right and The Rock in front of us and a little to Port, we were in the entrance to the Mediterranean Sea. Signals started flying about. The OOW was trying to tune his wireless radio into the news and the rumour mill was alive with words like; 'Argy's', 'Falklands', 'Bastards!'

WHAT?? The Argentinians?? I was pretty sure that they were a South American race, who live an awful long way from the Outer Hebrides. The Outer Hebrides were where we all assumed The Falkland Islands lay! We had never even heard of The Falkland Islands, I don't think anyone had! I stayed on the bridge as The Rock grew closer, because I wanted to know what was going on. I was ready for another run ashore! Surely we could have had a few pints before we go, couldn't we?

Big D came up from his cabin onto the Bridge, hair freshly Brylcreamed, "morning Riley, what's going on then?" "erm, the Argentinians Sir, the news, erm, The Falklands?" He of course knew already exactly where The Falklands were, he wasn't best pleased and he was very serious. The shit hit the fan basically. His experience took over immediately, he obviously knew what he was going to do.

He instructed the OOW to 'about turn' one hundred and eighty degrees and set a course back out of The Straits, turn left at Tangiers, then head south for EIGHT FUCKING THOUSAND MILES!! It was going to take us over two weeks at full ahead to get us there, we were going to go to war... WAR?

Big D addressed the ships Co. over the Tannoy and let us know that the Argentinians had invaded The Falkland Islands and raised the Argentinian flag in Port Stanley and on South Georgia. We were one of the most southerly ships with the others from Op ST, so off we were going with HMS Sheffield, HMS Glamorgan, (AKA 'Glamourous Organ') HMS Antrim and RFA Tidespring. We were the 'Spearhead Group', he didn't of course have all of the information available, it was coming through gradually and he would update us with anything we needed to know as soon as he did. The rest of the Task Force as it was later named was back home and they were about ten days behind us.

Everything then, seemed to be, on a 'need to know basis' and we obviously 'didn't need to know'. We started doing defence watches, which meant even less sleep than usual basically, as we set a course for Ascension Island. A tiny island in the middle of the ocean eight degrees south of the Equator. As we sailed south we continued exercising with the other ships, sailing in formations, sending signals by light, flag and short range radios from ship to ship keeping us all really busy.

By now we were on watch for up to nineteen hours a day and grabbing sleep whenever possible, sometimes in the mast, safe from Mal Banfield's indiscretions (mucky git!). This was a period of unknown really, we didn't of course have any way of knowing what was going on, other than the odd briefing. The internet hadn't even been thought of and Google wasn't in the English Oxford Dictionary. Pretty soon we were a thousand miles away from anywhere! I suppose we just got on with it, hours and hours on watch.

I filled some time in with cartoon drawing, which got me into some trouble once. I'd pinned some up on the noticeboard. One cartoon was slagging off people who weren't watch keepers who got to sleep all night in their bunks. They'd get up early for breakfast and scoff everything before we had finished our watch. I'd wander down after an early watch to find fuck all left. Hence the cartoons. One with the PO Chef saying, "my boy's 'ave been up since 'arf five!" (Luxury!). And

"Where's all the veg Chef?" – "In the bleedin' pies".

To slightly alter a Monty Python sketch; I'd been up since half an hour before they went to bed! (Google 'The Four Yorkshire men' genius!).

As we sailed further and further south, our Windies trip became less likely and if it hadn't resolved itself before a certain date / latitude then it would be cancelled and another ship from the 6th Frigate Squadron would actually steal OUR Windies jolly! We were obviously gutted as that date / latitude quickly passed, I'm not sure if anyone got it to be fair, I hope not anyway.

8th April 1982.

The Russians seem to be interested in our activities by flying close by in Bear Deltas. They were the huge planes with a massive radar domes on the top. *They were no doubt trying to intercept something of interest to them, from all of our transmissions.*

The weather was brilliant by now, it was absolutely boiling. Flying fish (they really do) shoot out of the water and completely clear the deck and dive in on the other side. Some didn't judge it too well, so they'd flap about on deck like they were having convulsions until they got near the side and back in they'd go, incredible! We were about two thousand miles away from land by now, except for Ascension that was two days away. It made you feel very small, just a dot floating in the middle of the Atlantic two miles deep.

It was on one of these days when word was sent round that a 'Splash Target Bosun' was needed and volunteers could apply. A splash target is exactly what it say's on the tin, a target that you can shoot at with the mortars or small arms. Now someone ACTUALLY applied to be the Splash Target Bosun. They got a splash target, basically a large float about four feet square, it had a hole in the middle so when it was dragged on a long line from the rear of the ship, the water would shoot up through the hole so that you could see it easily. I really can't remember who it was that was stupid enough to actually volunteer for such a task, but they got him ready in a wet suit and were giving him instructions of how to sit on the target. They actually blew it because they were laughing so much and the poor volunteer eventually twigged that it was a massive blag!

No! It wasn't me!!

10th April 1982.

We reached Ascension Island with the Glamorous Organ and Sheffield and anchored off the *island. Tidespring and Antrim also joined us.*

It was quite windy when we got thero, still hot though with a clear sky. The sea was absolutely filled with deadly creatures swimming about, you could see Hammer Head Sharks! Just swimming about, waiting for some easy to get scran. Some of the lads got fishing lines out, I remember Doc Peddy had a bucket that he'd caught some of these Pilot Fish in, they had a fearsome set of teeth, related to the Piranha apparently. He tried to pull the hook out of one, even their fins were sharp. He couldn't get the hook out, he pulled harder and its whole jaw, with teeth came out! It was a miniature of those trophy shark jaws you see hanging from walls in fishmongers and the occasional pub by the sea side. These fish would hang around the toilet outlets and have a feeding frenzy on any turds that were ejected. We'd throw apples and other bits of food in and the water would boil until it was completely gone. It was really funny, we used to look over the side, with an outlet below, just under the waterline. First some bubbles would shoot out as someone having dump had flushed, and we'd say "ooh look! A turd's coming..." Then the turd would shoot out and they'd swoop in at high speed for the kill and devour it in seconds.

The sharks weren't interested in any of that stuff, I think they were waiting for one of us! Shame we couldn't go for a swim really, apart from the beasties in there it looked really inviting and it was warm too.

Apart from stores and ammunition at Ascension we also took onboard, S.A.S. and S.B.S. personnel. We also took Taff back on board. We'd had enjoyed a little freedom without him as he had been stranded in Gib because we didn't come back of course. So he ended up getting a lift on our sister ship HMS Yarmouth. During his voyage to Ascension the ships Co. were ordered to 'shave off'. They weren't allowed to keep any beards also known as 'a set' or a 'full set' because of the problem that respirators or gas masks wouldn't work very well with hair between the skin and the rubber seal. When he got back onboard we hardly recognised him but fell about laughing at him because he was mortified to find that none of us had shaved for a couple of weeks. Apparently we didn't foresee a Nuclear, Biological or Chemical threat so we were free to grow away. My effort was pathetic!

11th April 1982.

We sailed from Ascension in the morning and got prepared for a long boring trip down south. Replenishing fuel and stores on *the way down with RFA's Appleleaf, Tidespring and Fort Austin.*

A 'R.A.S.' (Replenishment At Sea) was always good, a huge RFA (Royal Fleet Auxiliary ship) would come alongside us. We'd fire lines from rifles over to the RFA, the lines were attached to larger ropes and they'd attach them to the fuel lines. We'd then pull the lines across and fill our tanks up with the fuel. Supplies of food and drink came over along with ammunition and we would form long queues passing the boxes from one to another all along the deck, down ladders, down the main drag to the various store rooms. A split box containing stationary wasn't much fun but when the odd bar of nutty fell out that was better and it would cause a scurry, like flies (or Pilot fish) round shit.

Tommy Doak would show off his far superior light reading skills, there would be some old salt on the RFA that he knew from the old days and they'd flash messages to each other using the Aldis's, faster than I could read it. They'd even exchange the odd word using Semaphore with no flags, just hand movements. I tried to learn Semaphore with Steve McGarry once, but we learned the alphabet the wrong way round, so we put that one back to bed because if we had tried to use it, we would have been 'backing talkwards' and left the recipient very confused.

It was quite exhilarating cutting through the waves with a ship three times your size alongside, just thirty or forty feet away, you wouldn't want to fall between the two. I remember Big D going over to another warship using the same procedure on a Bosun's Chair once, he was winched across, he must have been crazy and you wouldn't catch me doing

THAT! He could have been Roger's stunt double after all!

We remained in a very open 'Sector Screen' formation to prevent detection by any merchant ships that may be gathering information on us in what we we're now called; 'The Task Force'.

We did a figure of 8 over the equator.

Over the next few days the weather gradually started to get colder and we met HMS Endurance, the by-now famous exploration ship that had been studying penguins and icebergs down on South Georgia. We met at sea with huge cheers between us, they had been lucky and got away and they only had a few Marines onboard and no real fire power. They did have a Wasp helicopter, they were really happy to see us, we were happy to see them safe too. With Antrim & Tidespring we headed towards the bleak outpost of South Georgia. At this point I noted in the diary; *'not much is known about what is going on or what we will do when we get there'*. I formed the opinion that the Islands, although I'd never heard of them before, (nor had anyone else) were British. There was a British colony living on there and they have pubs and red post boxes. OK, they're quite near Argentina, but they're BRITISH. It's like having a very long back yard and some fucker moves into your shed and nicks your lawn mower. Well I'm sorry mate but FUCK OFF!

Quite what we were going to do when we got there was a bit of a mystery. We'd got all these guys sleeping on our mess deck, on the floor, they were plied with our beer rations and we exchanged all sorts of tales. There were a few lads from the S.A.S. they were incredible, quite small, but packed solid, lean and strong. I remember watching them doing these sit up exercises on the fo'c's'le, they'd sit on the edge of a four foot square air conditioning outlet, with someone holding their feet. From the sitting position they'd drop back till their head almost touched the deck, with their hands behind their heads and pull themselves back up to the sitting position again. They had stomachs like cobblestone streets.

We had a good couple of weeks with those guys, they were every bit of what you see on the telly.

So you can only imagine what the mess was like with twenty seven of us and I can't remember how many more, kipping on your bunk (when you weren't in it) or kipping on the floor.

Going down into the mess in the middle of the night, you had to prepare yourself for the smell as you lowered yourself in. Sliding down the ladder the stink intensified as you got to the bottom and your feet landed on the deck. Think; the smell of all possible human gasses and bodily fluids, mixed up, then multiply that hum by ten.

One of the really funny things that we used to do to get them all laughing with us when the lights went out, was Spider's Spaghetti Western theme tune. When the lights were out you couldn't see a thing, everyone would settle down and start to go off to sleep, of course we knew what was coming. Our guests on the deck didn't. He'd cup his hands together as if he was going to make an owl hooting noise, that annoying thing that some uncles do at weddings for the kids. Instead of the owl noise, he did this Spaghetti Western intro;

"oohweeeooohwwweeooooooohhh!" Then we'd all shout really loud in unison - "NAH NAAH NAAAH!"
"oohweeeooohwwweeooooooohhh!" (Up a key) "NAH NAAH NAAAAAAH!" Before long we'd all be NAH NAAARING on the queue of Spider in the back gulch. There wasn't really an ending to it as we'd go on for as long as we could before laughing brought it to a close. It certainly took your mind off things for a while. Then just as you were dropping off and in twitching mode in the silence…
"oohweeeooohwwweeooooooohhh" and off we'd all go again, "NAH NAAH NAAAAAAAH!"

The next two weeks were spent doing all sorts of emergency exercises, man over boards, fire drills, flood drills and chemical attack drills. We were given two dog tags made out of some fibre material. A maroon one and a dark green one. They were circular about the same size as a ten pence piece. They had your name, number and blood group on. We were given a chemical attack kit that we had to keep in our respirator bags that you'd have to administer to yourself in the event of one. If the signal was given for a gas or chemical attack, you'd have to use it. It was a stubby plastic cylinder with a cap on one end. You had to grip it in your hand and bang it down on your thigh, a huge needle would spring out and stab into your leg, releasing some anti-chemical attack agent, probably cyanide as that would be a more comfortable demise! And anyway how would they know what anti-chemical chemical to give us, when they wouldn't know what chemical we were infected with… or did they? There was also a massive pill that we'd have to take too, if there was any sign of an N.B.C.D. 'D' for Defence. This we were told could come in the form of droplets from the air, a bit frightening really… really? Could that really happen? The ship was covered in sprinklers too, to wash the upper deck down in an attack. I didn't want to think about it really and stuff like that I put to the back of my mind.

We were also advised to write a will. I was twenty, there was no way I was going to write a will! That has put me off writing one since, I really must get around to it one day.

We were in defence watches all the time by now and it was getting extremely cold, I've never seen waves so big. Some were estimated at sixty footers! (Girt Great Goffers!). We were in an area called the Forties, or the Roaring Forties. For some reason I was never sea sick again. Anyway we were ploughing through these waves and at times it was quite frightening, it was like my previous explanation multiplied by three! 'Shipping it green' was when the nose, dived so deep into the next wave after the last, that a thirty to forty foot wall of solid sea would seem to shoot up vertically and within a second it would slam onto the bridge windows, incredible!

During one of these storms, I was asleep on my bunk and sometimes the ship veers to port or starboard if the wave pattern isn't even, or if the ship is going on a course across the waves. I suddenly found myself separated from my bunk and in mid-air. I'd been tossed a couple of inches up from my mattress and then the ship veered, leaving me in mid-air, like the Roadrunner (meep meep!) just before the deck came up to meet me with a slap on my back, ooof! That'd knock the wind out of you!

Trying to keep warm when working on the upper deck was another problem, so out came the jeans under your number eight's. We were given cold weather clothing, which just went on top of what you already had on. We had submariners white polo neck wool jumpers, body warmers, thick socks, thin socks, I looked twice the size. Plus being at Action Stations a lot of the time, if you were only going to get a couple of hours in your pit you'd leave it all on, except your Steaming Bats (ridiculous looking steel toe capped boots).

Eggs had probably finished by about now and milk was just UHT, quite a few things were running out. We were allowed either a slice of bacon or a sausage, not both! Of course the caterers were having to do other duties, fire exercises etc. too, so the nose bag suffered. They didn't have as much time to prepare the usual cuisine so Corn Dog Hash became the norm most days, anyway who doesn't like that with brown sauce? Ironically it was made from Argentinian Corned Beef!

21st April 1982.

First icebergs sighted at 10:40z time, we were on our own clock now, Zulu time.

Rather than messing with time zones we stuck to 'Zulu time' which was just Greenwich Mean Time rather than local time.

The first iceberg was an amazing sight white topped, massive, with a brilliant blue shimmer underneath. You could smell them and hear them, it was like they were alive. They smelt of cold, strangely, and creaked and groaned. One we saw on the radar was estimated as being eleven miles across! Watching out for rouge bergs, or 'Growlers' that were just under the water was a job that now needed to be done. Handily you could do that while looking out for Argentinian subs.

BBC World Service was our only link to Blighty now...

23rd April 1982.

Possible Guppy class submarine in the area.

I don't know if this was the same time that we depth charged a sighting of a possible sub with the mortars or not. I went aft to have a look, obviously oil would come to the surface first then bodies and other stuff if we had hit a submarine. Blood and guts from a poor whale was all that surfaced.

Endurance was detached to South Georgia. I think with our guests on board to do their thing. *We headed north to meet RFA Brambleleaf.*

25th April 1982.

I remember a massive snow storm that literally covered the upper deck within minutes, there was also an Argentine Sub, the Santa Fe. It was damaged somehow due to weather, alongside in Grytviken the old whaling station.

At 09:30 we were at uction stations going 30 knots to go in and 'get him', bloody hell we were going in for the kill, for real! Our Wasp helicopter and Antrim's Lynx took off and went into Grytviken and destroyed it.

(It was actually Brilliants lynx!).

During a lull in Grytviken, a bay with an abandoned whaling station in the distance and a huge glacier slithering its way down the mountain. When I first saw the glacier, I thought wow! Then I realised just how big it was when compared to the mountains that it was passing between, it was immense!

To assist the ground forces we did some N.G.S.'ing (firing four point five inch shells at their land forces positions to assist our ground troops). When Antrim went in again their white flag was flying.

The S.A.S. must have done the clearing up job, we had General Astiz escorted onboard to sign the surrender. He was escorted at gun point by some angry looking Boot Necks right behind me on the bridge and he was taken to the Wardroom under arrest where he signed the surrender of South Georgia. It was now British again.

Big D & Capt'n Barker from Endurance taking the surrender in our wardroom. Al's photo.

It can't go on for long now surely, there is however the problem that they invaded the Falkland Island itself and more of our troops and ships were on their way there too.

The S.A.S. lads got us a present as a 'thank you' for putting them up. I was on the bridge when I saw a helicopter coming towards us, it had a big rope sack slung underneath it. As it got closer, I could see that it was going to drop whatever it was carrying onto the fo'c's'le, it slowly lowered its cargo to the deck. The cargo had antlers! Some of the lads dragged it free and the helicopter took off again with a wave from the pilot. It was a full size Stag! Gutted! The Stag that is, not me. I went down to have a look at him and took some photos. His belly had been slit open and innards cleaned out. His purple tongue was hanging out and his eyes were open. There was a bullet wound on his neck… DINNER! The Chefs strung him up on the mortars to drain him. A few unfortunates had the fright of their lives when going out for a breather in the dark when they walked into him. He was later butchered and I had a chop!

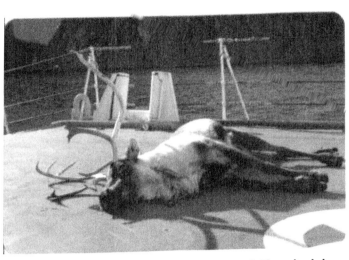

Rudolph. His antlers adorned the bridge roof for a few years till they went missing.

1st May 1982.

By now we were feeling pretty good, we'd got South Georgia back, (basically a fucking great ice bucket) *and now we just had to get the rest of the islands back and from now on we wouldn't be on our own. Most of the fleet was on its way, so we were sent north to meet them, to escort them back in.*

(On the 1st of May). *We were detached from the Invincible group and headed back to South Georgia, we were still some distance away and safe, it was all quiet at sea.*

We remained at sea till, I noted, the 41st day (8 May) when we were heading north to meet the LSL's, (Sir Percival, Sir Geraint and Sir Galahad) to escort them to the Falklands. We met up with the S.S. Uganda, the hospital ship during the first watch, passing a few signals to each other. It used to be a ship that school kids used to go on school trips in.

We'd been at sea for quite some time by now and there was the slightest chance that there would have been some nurses on that ship!

(Female ones). My binoculars were hot property for a while, "giz a go mate!" You couldn't see any nurses of course, far too cold for sunbathing. She went on her way during the night.

I hadn't actually noted it in the book but HMS Sheffield was hit by an Exocet on this day, I remember the message over the Tannoy, telling us what had happened. I was drinking a can of Courage Ale at the time... We just looked at each other - stunned...

9th May 1982.

In the early morning the LSL's are found and we are in company with Antrim, we met up with twenty other ships that included the huge white cruise ship Canberra and started to head back down South in a huge formation. People are getting a little nervous now, Sir Galahad said she'd spotted an aircraft to be presumed hostile, but it was a satellite and the possible gunfire was lightening. Exercise Action Stations every other day.

10th May 1982.

Sheffield sank whilst under tow...

17th May 1982.

We met up with the Hermes group and the radio is starting to get busy as usual.

I remember calling the Hermes on UHF and authenticating the signal to make sure from a code that we were talking to the right people and not just a well-spoken Argentinian. I knew exactly who I was talking to, it was Nick Payne, and I recognised his voice and accent. I used the letters November Papa for him to send a corresponding letter back to authenticate who he was, and then he sent back my initials for me to authenticate. He joined a couple of weeks after me and Wally, we all went to the same school. Summerhill Comprehensive in Kingswinford.

19th May 1982.

We are at present wandering round the group, around the Tactical Exclusion Zone (coiled springs) bored really.

During the long first watch, one of HMS Intrepid's Sea King helicopters ditched and there are quite a few men missing.

It turned out that the missing men were our S.A.S. guests, who had presented us with Rudolph. They'd crashed into the sea, some malfunction or other, in the pitch dark, I'm not sure if any survived. That was a kick in the teeth, we didn't even know any of their names. They never told us their names...

The thought of drowning in sea water sent shivers through my spine. The water was only still in liquid form because it had salt in it. You wouldn't survive more than a minute or two in that! This reality was a distinct possibility for us now too.

21st May 1982.

We secure alongside HMS Argonaut they'd just taken a pounding in what we now called Bomb Alley (San Carlos Bay). The ship had no propulsion but her weapons were still working.

The air attacks have started and we are now patrolling around looking out all the time for enemy air craft.

They were coming in the form of Daggers, A5's. The pilots were brave men indeed, facing all of our guns, they did have the element of surprise and definitely speed on their side. There were hills all around the edge of San Carlos Bay with an opening at the southern end into 'The Gap', the stretch of water between the two parts of the Island. They would come in with little warning as our radars were limited by the hills so we had to rely on visual most of the time. They used to streak across the landscape, attacking whoever they could, as they were being fired at by everything all the ships there had. There were Sea Cat missiles firing off, machine guns blattering, four five's booming, the lot. Some jets I saw streaking across the bay over the beach would just stop dead in a millisecond from 500mph and in a small cloud of smoke, disintegrate into bits that would just land on the hillside smoking.

We took the lads onboard from Argonaut, they all had blackened faces from the smoke, they'd had a fire onboard and there was a live 1,000lb bomb in her engine room.

The lads were visibly shaking, most probably suffering from shock, we led some down to the dining hall to get some breakfast, none of them said much at all.

We took their two young, dead sailors onboard for Doc to prepare for burial, Iain Boldy and Matthew Stuart. Iain had just got married the week before he left England and Stuart had just turned eighteen the day before, so I was told. A couple of days later, when out at sea, the whole ships company was gathered onto the flight deck and the quarter deck for their burial at sea. The night was pitch black, just about everyone was there looking down on the two Union flags that were draped over their bodies, illuminated by a couple of bulbs rigged up that bathed them in a dim light. They were wrapped up like Egyptian mummies under the flags. There were two Padres, they didn't need microphones or have to shout, it was silence except for sniffing noses and breathing. They read passages from their Bibles in turn and on the nod their bodies on wooden boards, were lifted from the head end. A small patch of water was lit by the lighting. They slipped from under the flags and over the side, landing in the water feet first. The white of the wrapping showed as they went down the first few feet then, as the ripples of the water contorted their outlines, they went silently out of sight into the depths. I often think about standing there, staring into the water where they went to their graves at the bottom of the ocean. (To those still on patrol, I salute you).

Nothing recorded in the book but this was the afternoon when HMS Ardent was hit too, we were in the sound, Ardent was a few miles away from us. They were attacked countless times, by different planes, I can't remember what types. If you Google it, it tells you, I know it does but I can't face reading stuff like that. Once they'd scored a hit and damaged her they kept coming in for the kill, over and over, the ship exploded. There were fires all over the place, there was nothing we could do, Yarmouth was near and took on some survivors but 22 men didn't come home that day. We watched the Ardent burn and explode all night while we were tied up alongside Argonaut. It was awful.

22nd May 1982.

The sun came up at around 1030z time, so we had to be prepared, we'd go to action stations. Sleep was now at a premium, I hadn't slept more than a couple of hours over the last couple of days and the thought of going for a shower was furthest from my mind.

From a deep sleep I'd be up on the bridge at the sound of the alarm, pen in hand within ninety seconds.

On one occasion I had got undressed to sleep and in my panic when the alarm sounded, I woke up, jumped out of my scratcher in the dark and put Taff's trousers on by mistake. I ran up to the bridge! On the way up I thought, bit odd... I realised once I'd got there that I was wearing a pair of extremely baggy trousers. It's not like I could have gone back to get changed, as we were expecting an air raid any minute. His action station was in the wheel house, just down the ladder from the bridge, he shouted up "Spike!" I looked down, he was stood there in his Reg Grundies, holding up my trousers, a quick exchange took place there and then.

It's funny looking at the diary now, the way that I just wrote the notes in such a matter-of-fact way, never knowing that I'd probably want to remember these details from it one day. So inevitably there will have been so much that I didn't write down that I'll have forgotten forever, the same as all of the photos that I didn't take.

1038z at action stations ready for the Spicks hoping to sign off watch tonight, the beer chit is in.

(Hoping to sign off watch tonight). That meant that I was there on the bridge and hoping that the worst wouldn't happen before darkness fell and the raids would stop because I'd put the beer chit in and I was in need of a few tinnies. By now the reality of death was becoming all too serious, these Argies were actually trying to kill us and we were trying to kill them! Sometimes it was like watching a very intense football match (I can imagine). If the action wasn't too close to us, we'd be shouting support for the other ships, firing at the planes and when one was hit, it was;

"YEEAAAH!"

1700z LRO Todd & Ro Riley have been on watch all the time. Wandering around San Carlos Water, Argonaut is still U/S.

Beers & ZZZZZZZZZZZ!

24th May 1982.

On the bridge ready for action stations, we have just come back into San Carlos Water 1153 and the sun is just up. Antelope is slowly burning away in the background. Arrow and Yarmouth are nearby.

The previous day I'd been on watch on the bridge, I had my old Cannon AV1 SLR camera, with a 75mm x 200mm lens attached. It was sat on the desk most of the time as usual, when two Daggers came over the hillside on the opposite side to us, from the West at a guess, towards us. Yarmouth and Antelope were the first two ships they would have seen, the ships opened fire, and bombs were dropped. The first jet suddenly upturned and blew up. It split in two just as I clicked the shutter, the two pieces on fire, dropping into the sea, the second one turned a sharp left and headed north out of there. The pilot was pulled out of the water later, very dead. His plane had struck the Yarmouth's mast as he was being filled with bullets, he dropped a couple of one thousand pounders, one of which went into the side of Antelope.

To the right, plumes of water from 1,000lb'ers he'd dropped. Two parts of the plane just before they hit the water.

Yarmouth in the spray and smoke, Antelope in the foreground.

Below is the same picture, if you look just to the right there is a small dark triangle just left of the wiper blade. He's the one that got away but headed straight for a type 22 (probably HMS Broadsword).

The Antelope limped further into the bay with smoke coming from the funnel, they started to get the men off as it got dark, then all of a sudden BOOOM! The bomb went off as Staff Sergeant Jim Prescott and WO John Phillips were defusing it. Jim was killed instantly, John lost his arm. I didn't know that then obviously, we were concerned with looking for anyone in the water. I managed to get a photo of Antelope just after the explosion, which I believe John has a large copy of in his garden, care of Alan Titchmarsh.

Antelope just after the explosion.

We are positioned about a mile and a half from the bay entrance (a very dangerous place to be because they would fly up the Sound for cover and come through the gap).

Waiting for the Argies. There is no cloud cover on our side. They should be in for a bit of trouble today, we are ready and waiting. Further sitrep follows when it's dark!

25th May 1982.

0200z Long morning watch, about 6 Argie planes were shot down yesterday and Sir Geraint was the only ship to be damaged with a (British Made 1,000lb UXB).

We found out at about this time that these bombs they were using were British made and bought up by the Argentinians after WWII. Also it turned out that they weren't priming them properly, they were set for a higher launch, but because they had to fly very low to avoid our radar, they were dropping them and they weren't exploding. Not that we were going to give them any advice on that subject!

0630 At sea ATT (can't remember what that meant, although it could be At This Time) *with Tidepool, Broadsword and Yarmouth. S.S. Uganda in sight for a R.A.S. and a boat transfer with HMS Ambuscade. We will be back in San Carlos water for sunrise the same as yesterday.* I also noted that *the 25th*

May is a big day for the Argies so they may have a last fling at us.

0800 RO Riley off.

1030 at action stations again, Antelope smoking gently at the far end of the bay when she slowly split in two and slipped into the water...

Pretty quiet till PM. Anchorage attacked by 4 Skyhawks, 2 shot down by Yarmouth.

Coventry is also doing well today - has shot down 2 Argies with Sea Dart.

When there was time for rest, I'd lie there on my bunk, stinking, I hadn't had a shower for weeks. I could smell myself, the smell in the mess intensified, not JUST because of me! Hygiene had taken a bit of a back step. I was alright if I didn't take all my layers off, but when it came to a regular necessity to clear the tubes when possible, the hum became apparent. Still needs must! I don't think any of us would disagree with me there! If they do they're lying, but they're not the sort to be bashful!

I also remember at around this time only on one occasion thinking to myself that this is going to go horribly wrong at some stage, we have had Lady Luck on our side for far too long. We'd been in the thick of it for a while now and so far we were unscathed. I'm not a religious man but I did say a little selfish prayer to myself one night and quietly cried myself to sleep, thinking of home, I wasn't sure if I'd ever get back there.

Spending hours in Bomb alley, I could see the beach on the East shore that we were nearest for most of our time there. It was probably half a mile away, if the ship did sink, and you managed to get most of your layers of clothes off, it may be possible to swim it before freezing to death.

There was a lone penguin. Most days he was there, I could see him through my binos, just standing there, he must have thought, 'what the fuck are they playing at? Noisy bastards!'

The Chief Chippy, whose name escapes me, looked like Bryan Ferry, was a fucking brave bastard. He for some reason had the job of manning the laser that had been mounted to the bridge roof. He was surrounded by sandbags containing gravel, rocks and sand. Eric the Rock was in there too. (I'll tell you about him in a bit). The laser was apparently top secret and we weren't to mention it for at least twenty five years, so it should be safe to mention it now. It was like a gun and operated by the counterbalancing weight of the Chippy who would swing it around and dispense a green laser beam towards any approaching enemy aircraft. Presumably to blind the pilot. He was there through all the air raids, in the open with no protection at all! I didn't hear of any pilots being blinded, but we did, as a combined effort, shoot down quite a few.

Knotty and Hutch were manning the Starboard Oerlikon, a 20mm cannon (a massive machine gun) that Hutch's weight would swing about in order to line up the crosshairs on the enemy and shoot at them, while Knotty loaded it with bullets.

Between them they filled a few planes with lead and both were mentioned in dispatches. In reality, it didn't matter if you were in the open or inside really because if a bullet had your name on it, it would pass through just about anything to get to you. We even joked about having our own bullets with our own names engraved on them to keep in our pockets.

26th May 1982.

1030 At action stations again all day, Coventry's day was not so good, she has now sunk. Atlantic Conveyor hit by two Exocet but still floating.

1439 Nothing happened yet but bridge swept out coz Big D asked me to. Closed up as usual from 1030 to approx. 2200 anchored in San Carlos with Fearless and

Arrow abreast us waiting for air raids.

Fri 28th May 1982.

On watch 0800 - 2200.

1045 @ action stations.

Yesterday was all quiet until dusk when they decided to descend on us. They attacked when it was nearly dark, (a cunning plan) when our CAP (Sea Harriers circling at 25,000') had gone. There were some casualties ashore, apparently the raid was aimed at land forces more than us in the bay but they still had a go at us! Today we expect much the same, a very boring day till *about 2000 but let's not count our eggs! Good cloud cover.*

Knotty's 19th Birthday.

Knotty was strangely late for his watch that evening, he was nowhere to be found. He hid in the Seaman's mess, where they surrounded him with their share of their beers and he got absolutely shiters! We covered for him, it was the least we could do. Only Knotty could manage to celebrate in style under fire!

A bit of a gap here, no entries in the diary, I can only assume it was business as usual…

Sat 29th May 1982.

1030 action stations. One aircraft over flew us yesterday above cloud level. Today so-far we have had no air raids, but plenty of false alarms as usual.

Still all quiet. The day is sunny with a blue sky but cold and windy with good visibility.

30th May 1982.

At present we are with the Hermes group outside the AOA(?) (Not in the muck and bullets probably). *For our so called 'holiday', most of the day has been taken up by Vertreps but no mail!*

I can't for the life of me remember what the hell a Vertrep was, but I remember the lack of mail. Sometimes we used to get letters delivered by helicopter that had been dunked in the oggin at some point (the mail, not the helicopter). (I've since found out that a Vertrep was of course a 'vertical replenishment', hence helicopter...) I'd spend hours writing letters to Mum & Dad, Dave & Paul and lots to my Gran, who I seemed to be able to pour my heart out to. I haven't used any of those letters for reference, they're about somewhere, but I've never been able to bring myself to read them. I do remember that Dave and I used to write to each other totally in Black Country! 'Owm ya gooin' oer kid?'

I used to take photos of any action I saw, if I managed to get to my camera in time and wasn't on the radio. I could sometimes use the camera while talking on the radio as there was a foot switch for transmitting with, a 'Prestel switch'. I had to be very selective over what I took photos of, I never knew when I'd run out of film or how much I'd need as I didn't know how long we were going to be there for, it was expensive too. I didn't have any spare rolls of film as I had to rely on the free films Truprint would send with the developed ones. I'd got some rolls that I'd brought with me but not many. That's hard to imagine now as you can take as many pictures as you like now on a digital camera. I used to send the films off for developing, from the ship in B.F.P.O. mail and they'd come back about three weeks later if I was lucky, although I think a few went missing in transit. I remember taking a few action shots that never materialised.

1640 went to action stations, suspected Exocet raid but it was a spurious radar contact.

Now THAT I really do remember! The thought of an Exocet was the most frightening as their Super Etendards had sunk the Sheffield and Atlantic Conveyor. The Super Etendards were French fighter jets with Exocet missiles strapped to them. They could also operate at night, so there was no chance of seeing them, it would be a hit with virtually no warning and lethal. I had to go down the bridge wing for something, for what I can't remember, but as I walked past the 2" Chaff launchers (big tubes that fires a rocket that explodes sending aluminium paper fluttering around in the air to confuse an incoming missile's radar, so hopefully it would miss).

WHOOOOSH! WHOOOOSH! WHOOOOSH!

I hit the deck like my legs had suddenly evaporated, "aaaaaaarrgh!" the noise was deafening! I thought we'd been hit but it was the Chaff rockets firing off! Right next to me, no warning, I absolutely shit myself! Turned out I wasn't the only one who thought we'd been hit, we'd never seen the Chaff rockets being fired off before, I suppose they must have been expensive and so only used sparingly.

1730 went to action stations again, two Exocets were fired from the enemy. We were near them I think. Everybody onboard was really scared. One missile was shot down by HMS Avenger, the other one missed everybody due to stax of chaff in the air. We were attacked by two Super Etendards, one was splashed by Exeter's Sea Dart. "Oh boy is this great!" (Some rest period).

2230 at action stations again, nothing happened.

A'noon 31 May D day + 10

Not too busy at the moment. Still with the Hermes and Invincible group. About to R.A.S. with RFA Fort Austin, can't get her on Tac (U.H.F. Tactical Radio). The boarding of an Argie Hospital ship called off, we're going back to Bomb Alley instead!

1st June 1982.

0200 All quiet but rough. We are about eight miles away from the rest, still in UHF range, for maintenance on the four five's.

0800 Tac UHF as usual, boring stuff from Hermes (Nick Payne, well not him personally, he just had to transmit it.) R.A.S.(S) is taking place ('S' for stores) at 1100. THAT will be really great..."clear lower deck" to make it even greater! I even put 'sarcasm' in brackets there. It was all getting a little too much to bear.

Evening: - back on our way to Bomb Alley.

2nd June 1982.

Well, we are back in down town Bomb Alley after our well-earned holiday!? And should be closed up at action stations till 2200ish tonight. We will have to watch out for customised Sea King helo's that carry Exocets!

3rd June 1982.

Very quiet no air raids.

4th June 1982.

We are at anchor in Bomb Alley again, good cloud cover. Last night we fired 150 rounds over their heads at Port Howard, it was cut short due to bad visibility but it was reported to be accurate.

I remember that night because Big D had reasoned that there was no need for everyone to be at action stations to do the NGS'ing, as we were out of range for the enemy and firing into the distance, guided by some brave people on the ground who were watching where all the ordinance was landing.

So there I am, lying on my bunk, trying to sleep, with the clatter of machinery and shells in the bomb room below, the lads shouting and loading the bombs into the hoist, the noise of the hoist clattering the shells up to the loader under the gun and BANG!PING!BANG!PING!BANG!PING! X 150! Enough to drive you crazy!

All is quiet in the Bay, air threat is yellow, no mail in sight. We will probably carry on with more NGS'ing tonight. That's about it.

1935 air threat back to yellow, it went to red at approx. 1925 and 4-6 aircraft flew nearby. Not close enough for any ships to engage them. They dropped some bombs but nowhere near us. One aircraft was reported to have said on radio "I have run out of fuel". Comment: - Tough! That's all N.B. Cloud cover is very good and it's tippin' it down. Tonight is going to be spent as A.S.W. patrol ship (Anti-Sub Warfare?) (I've always been rubbish with abbreviations, why not just say it?). (FFS!).

We are at present patrolling up and down the sound. All quiet apart from the air raid at scran time but we didn't go to action stations.

All quiet now.

5th June 1982.

Just departed from Sir Percival at 0830 and we are on our way back. Exeter has hostile aircraft on her radar, 140 miles away and now lost them. 1100 Just entering San Carlos again and closed up at action stations. Somehow I think it's going to be the day.

1725 Nothing happened yet?

7th June 1982.

Everything as usual.

1155 the sun has come up and we have just dropped anchor in San Carlos Bay. Nothing different happened yesterday, fell out from action stations at 1930. (6th June).

1201 at action stations. An air raid is on its way from the N.W. (you know what N.W. means!)

1216 fallen out. 2 aircraft out of 3 splashed by Sea Dart. We never saw them until they exploded! One got away good ole Exeter! Correction there were only 2 Canberra's, one was darted and one got away. The rest of the day was quiet apart from 2 false alarms.

I remember one of those being shot down, I was stood watching as this bloody great rocket fired from Exeter's deck, burning all the paintwork as it shot off skywards, up, up, up, it went, up further, leaving an Apollo like smoke trail, till it was just a dot, there was another dot, they came together, a silent puff of smoke, then a few bits came out of the puff of smoke, carried on forwards for a bit, with smoke trailing then plummeted Earthwards. (Almost clinical). There was someone in that plane…

2100 Proceeding out to sea for the night as usual.

"Beam Me Up Scotty"

8th June 1982.

We'd been at action stations for most of that day and we were going to leave the Bay to fire some 4.5 inchers off to the other side of the islands where our land based spotters had identified an Argentinian observation post that was reporting our ships positions. I wasn't the only one who was nervous, we didn't venture into the Sound very often, especially before nightfall. Having witnessed HMS Ardent being attacked out there a couple of weeks before, made it very un-nerving. We also knew that Special Forces were in Argentina, spotting their aircraft taking off. So that gave us about half an hour before we had to get back to the relative safety of Bomb Alley. We headed for "The Gap", the sea was calm, and always a little rougher as you enter the sound as it's not protected by the Bay. As we nosed out through the Gap (from a distance the Gap only looked like a small space between the two headlands. It was actually probably about half a mile wide at a rough guess), we slowly moved out into the Sound, I looked to Port and instinctively shouted "SIR, ENEMY AIRCRAFT!" I could see five of them, coming straight for us from the East between the two halves of the Islands, they were at the same height as the headland, probably less than a hundred feet off the water. Really fast, those things can do over 500mph! "WHAT'S THE BEARING SIR?" he looked at the compass in the middle of the bridge and followed them as they zoomed past us, he said "TWO-SEVEN-ZERO" (they obviously weren't at 270 for long but anyway, I shouted my well-rehearsed codes for 'enemy aircraft bearing 270' on the tactical radio and watched them scream past in front of us and climb. They were probably just as surprised to see us as we were them! All hell let loose, alarms sounding, orders being shouted, Tannoy barking instructions, guys running around. The ship rolled heavily as the Captain ordered the ship to be turned about at full speed and head back into the relative safety of Bomb Alley. We were in big trouble, they had obviously seen us, we were a big target they probably even knew it was the Plymouth! I cricked my neck to look out of the window to my right as they climbed high and began to circle around to start their attack, they were Skyhawks. It was frantic, I grabbed my camera as the Tannoy barked "HIT THE DECK! HIT THE DECK!" I was determined to get some shots, so I didn't as we used to say; 'make like a coat of polish', I could see where they were coming from, and they swooped around to the left and came at us extremely quickly, I looked out of the open starboard bridge door as 30mm & 20mm cannon shells started to smash into the port side, some passing straight through, taking bits and pieces with them, spraying shrapnel and hitting the water on the starboard side, I pressed the foot pedal to transmit, lifted my camera to my eye and said over the radio "BEAM ME UP SCOTTY!" I took some photos as they dropped their cargo of 1,000lb bombs, two of them splashing in the water really close just off the starboard side. One went through the funnel and two through the quarter deck all ended up in the sea. The noise was incredible, every weapon on board was being fired at them 4.5's, SMG'S, GPMG'S, 9mm's, SLR'S and Seacat missiles. All you could smell was Cordite, like gunpowder smoke. Plain speak was not allowed on UHF and I wasn't spoken to about it later, I thought I might have got into trouble for it but I just thought fuck it, it was the first thing that came into my head. In any case we had more to worry about than that. We didn't know at first if they were going to come back to finish us off like they did with the Ardent. The Petty Officers mess and the dining hall were on fire and we were also beginning to list over to starboard, because of all the water they were using for firefighting that was sloshing around. Thick black smoke made its way along the main drag and up the two decks to the bridge past me and blasted out of the bridge door. A lad slumped at the top of the ladder up to the bridge, he was obviously shocked and he asked me if he was ok, I checked his head, he had a cut on his scalp somewhere but he was otherwise ok and kept his anti-flash hood on, I assured him that he'd be fine and he disappeared back into the smoke. The gunners spilled out of the four five turret, I could see them from my position through the window, looking down I saw Bob

Donkin, a big burly bloke, holding his hand, it was bleeding badly, looked like his thumb was hanging off, one of the other lads apparently had a broken arm. Bullets had pinged around inside the turret. The black smoke filled the bridge quickly, Taff's voice came up from the tiller house below and he shouted "someone chuck a gas mask down!" I grabbed my gas mask bag, but I was having difficulty breathing too, as the bridge was by now filled with this acrid dense black smoke. I pulled out the spare filter, a round black tin thing filled with charcoal that had a short stubby threaded tube on the other side that screws into the front of the gas mask, and I stuffed it in my mouth, I threw my gas mask with a filter attached in the bag, down to the ladder so that he could see and breathe... and steer the ship! We weren't supposed to use them for smoke but it seemed like the only option, in fact it worked quite well, but my eyes were streaming.

Eventually the threat from the air raid seemed to have passed, they didn't come back and have a go at us again saving us from a fate similar to the crew on the Ardent. The damage control parties managed to bring the fire and flooding under control, we still had power at least, so the prospect of having to swim half a mile to the shore to meet the lone penguin on the beach, seemed less of a reality all of a sudden. The whole episode made me feel that all of our training and practice down at Portland and Op Springtrain, was made for this day and it seemed to have paid off. The ship was a mess and five of our lads suffered injuries, some serious, thankfully none were fatal.

We had one bomb lodged down aft somewhere and once the fires were out and we were safely at anchor, virtually the whole ships company went up on deck at the pointy end, the safest place to be while the bomb disposal team got rid of it.

The planes, I've since heard from an Argentine contact on Facebook who I'm friends with, were called 'Los Gatos y Perros' squadron (Cats & Dogs). I was told we shot two down and damaged a Third.

The three surviving planes went on to Bluff Cove and attacked the Sir Galahad that was anchored there preparing to unload the troops. There was a big explosion and fire that killed and injured so many of the Welsh Guards and crew onboard, Simon Weston being one of the casualties, he was the worst injured man to survive. It could have been even worse if we hadn't shot two of them down before they got there. It's a pity we couldn't stop them all. Forty eight men didn't come home. I'm not sure when it was when we found out about what had happened to the Galahad, I am sure that it wouldn't have been straight away because as usual we wouldn't have needed to know.

I have also since learned that all of the pilots from the squadron Los Gatos y Peros survived to tell the tale. They were very brave men indeed.

We weren't raided again that day fortunately although we were worried that they might try to finish us off. The rest of the night was spent cleaning up. The holes were shored up and the water threatening to sink us was pumped back out. The fire was put out and all that was left was the stink of melted plastic.

When I was relieved from my action station I went with my camera for a walk about and took a few photos of the damage. There was a big entry hole in the port side of the funnel and a gaping exit wound with oil dripping down the other side of it, like it was wounded. There were holes all down the side of the ship, some you could see through from the inside-out. I went down aft and the stench of burnt plastic got worse, the dining hall was a blackened mess, there were orange misshapen blobs on four legs that used to be chairs, the two juice machines were melted into big solidified blobs, which looked like large lumps of discarded chewing gum. The rest of the room was blackened with solidifying great gooey drips coming from the deck head. (Ceiling... did I tell you that?) Next door was the Petty Officers mess, the fire had come from there. It was completely gutted. There was an AS12 Anti-submarine missile on the Flight Deck, just above the PO's mess that had exploded and made a hole in the deck down into the PO's mess, setting it on fire. It had probably been hit by a stray bullet.

Going out the back onto the quarter deck, just on the right, was a big split in the steel where a bomb had forced its way through, it pinged up and deflected off one of the mortar tubes folding the end of it in, then it carried on and ended up in the sea. Further aft on the bulkhead there was a 12" hole in the side of the ship where a bomb had passed right through, the ladder up to the flight deck was gone. So was the steel door leaving the compartment there open at the back. The door clips were left twisted as if they'd hung on to the door for as long as they could but it was just swiped from its hinges and their grasp.

I didn't know it at the time but my mate Jack Warner was being treated for his injury in the sick bay and a bible basher was giving him his last rites. He had an aluminium door hatch bracket stuck in his head and wasn't expected to survive. He was taken to the hospital ship with the others. He had 'hit the deck' in the main drag, when the raid came in. When the cannon shell hit the AS12 missile on the flight deck above and blew a hole in the deck, gutting the PO's mess, Jack was on the floor by the door to the mess and when the emergency exit hatch blew out, one of the clips securing it, hit him in the head.

I made my way up the other ladder on the starboard side up to the flight deck with the hole on the starboard edge of it. I went up the next set of ladders back to my part of ship, where people were clearing up bits of shrapnel and checking the damage. I went up to the signal deck, Stevie Mac said that he'd had a close shave and when I thought about it so had I. A few minutes before the air raid warning came in, I was with Steve on the signal deck, and in fact we'd been inside the mast. He showed me a hole on the side of the mast at the same level as the signal deck and his head, he was squatting down for cover just a couple of feet away. The hole had been caused by a 20 or 30mm Cannon shell. I looked inside the V/S store and it was a right mess. Tommy's 'white man's magic' was all over the place. The bullet had pinged around inside the compartment wrecking everything it hit. The golf clubs were all over the place with the shafts all twisted and his bike had been flung about. It had a huge dent in the yoke, where the bullet had ricocheted. All other bits and pieces were all over the place. The bullet ended up on the floor - all it was, was a little brass gnarled nugget. There were marks on the bulkheads where it had bounced around. He'd need white man's magic to fix it!

My diary says after all this that *it is thought that none of their planes that set out today got back. They were either shot down by Rapier, Sea Harriers or our 20mm (C/O Hutch & Knotty) and our Sea Cat'.* Then it say's *'So the Argies still came off worst. That's all'.* I wonder who started that rumour, well it made us feel better at the time anyway!

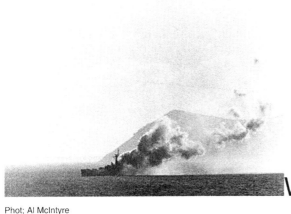

We're in trouble!

Phot; Al McIntyre

Close! Two that missed, smoke coming from his tail. Just to the left is our Sea Cat chasing after him. The smudge to the right is probably shrapnel from the funnel.

The last one going down (very faint) in the middle of the picture in the distance just above the horizon. The next one is on his way. Orange dot is a tracer bullet.

The hole in the quarter deck bulkhead, the steel peeled open.

Taken from where the ladder was. On the right you can see the twisted door clips.

The quarter deck damage and the second hole in the side.

The hole in the flight deck down to the PO's mess.

The hole in the funnel. The signal deck is just in front of the mast.

9th June 1982.

A lot of cleaning up is going on below decks, all fires are out. Stayed at anchor all last night cleaning up, all quiet today so far, only one false alarm, fingers crossed.

0300 10th June 1982.

R/V'd with Active and Atlantic Causeway and in a sector screen. Possibly on our way to Stena Seaspread, an oil rig repair ship.

11th June 1982.

We are with Stena Seapread for repairs by FMG. (Fleet Maintenance Group) but I remember coming alongside this thing, it was absolutely huge, it had a red hull and a white upper deck with a massive flight deck. They had skilled welders and engineers onboard who set to work on our damaged bits to get her fit to go back into battle again.

12th June 1982.

Still being repaired by FMG. N.G.S.'ing on Port Stanley? Repairs not expected to be complete until tomorrow.

Long First Watch (2000 - 0200).

In company with Glamorgan, she'd been involved in an Exocet attack, she's staying with us overnight to transfer stores and food etc.

She had a massive black hole just aft of amidships around the port side of the hangar and flight deck, I was told that they had fourteen dead. FOURTEEN! How fucking lucky were we?

It didn't bear thinking about, and we were going to go back in... So we didn't feel particularly lucky at all.

We, us and Glamorgan, parted company with big cheers on the upper deck, what must they have been thinking? We sailed off unfortunately having to go and bomb Port Stanley... and NOT go home. Morale very low.

DAY 78.

On bridge for action stations Long First 14 / 15 June 1982 @ 0113 THEY SURRENDERED!

What happened was that we met up with some other ships, I can't remember who now but I do remember getting up to 30 Knots, in choppy sea, from, if I'm right, about 30 odd miles out, I was on the bridge and we were at action stations and with the other ships we were on the attack. We were headed for Port Stanley and this was going to be it! We were advised as we were heading through a minefield at speed to stand with our knees bent. Just in case we hit a mine, having bent knees should in theory prevent your knee caps breaking! The low morale went straight out of the window, we were now more like "C'MAAAHN!" Then, at 0113z, we were just a few miles away from Port Stanley Harbour and we got word that they had surrendered.

We entered the Harbour, first ship in? I can't remember. We dropped the anchor about quarter of a mile away from the jetty, I could see through the binos, all of the Argy soldiers sat around, with piles of ammunition around them, people trudging about, they were defeated men. I couldn't see much more than that, some of our crew got to go ashore to do various tasks but really it was disappointment again by the 16th June because we were now Q.H.M. Port Stanley.

17th June 1982.

Not much happening just transferring people etc. to shore via our new boat HMS Oggie, renamed by Big H I think a little black tug boat.

Then - good news! 1955z Big D said we're shunting! Then I wrote; 'possibly' in brackets...

18th June 1982 - 82 days at sea.

In Port Stanley at anchor E.T.D. 0800 (it was raining heavily).

19th June 1982.

Back in San Carlos! Doing a water pump over with Elk and a R.A.S. with Blue Rover at 1000. Then after that, back to our normal anchorage, in view of the Gap. Had no air attacks today!

The Sea Rider (inflatable boat) was taking people ashore for a stretch of their legs. I watched Titch pick up the lone penguin for a photo through the binoculars.

We should be sailing for the main force at 22 or 2300 tonight to spend a quiet Sunday with them?!

20th June 1982. A'noon.

In company with the Hermes group, bye-bye San Carlos, still waiting for Glamorgan to catch up.

21st June 1982.

We have detached on a course of 061 speed 16.5 headed for Ascension with not so Glamorous

Organ on our Port beam - WE'RE OFF AT LAST!

22nd June 1982.

Getting further away from any air threat range.

LRO Hutch Hutcheson, RO1 Tadger & RO1 Knotty Ash.

23rd June 1982.

With Glam, 1000 miles N.E. of the Falklands!

Weather getting warmer.

24th June 1982.

Weather bad but quiet.

26th June 1982.

The sun's come out at last!

27th June 1982.

R.A.S. with R.F.A. Tamar, one of the petrol stations on the way. BBQ on the flight deck in the sun, with beer and steak and chips. 700 miles to Ascension.

28th June 1982.

Sods Opera night. All quiet up front, bedlam on the flight deck.

Left to right; Col Riley, Scotty, Sid & Hutch.

Sods Opera was a party. The flight deck was done up with a stage and everyone involved found all sorts of bits of clothing to make fancy dress costumes and they put on a show. I didn't get involved being my first one, plenty did though. Scotty was dressed as a punk, Foggy was a Spiv. Sid was dressed in a pink overall and a beret, I'm not sure why. Hutch was a compere for the beauty contest, where some of the Seamen upstaged us lot by dressing up as women and paraded up and down to great cheers from the audience. We were all drinking and having a great time, Hutch with hanky in hand and a black velvet jacket got Big D to judge the beauties. The winner of the competition by this time did actually look quite attractive... ahem! Another beauty had one of the officers lift his/her skirt up, he/she had no underwear on and he'd tucked his bits between his legs leaving a pubic triangle for authenticity! It was a scream! There were all sorts of other sketches that people had thought up and performed.

Enoch, Mal, Col, Foggie & Scotty. Sid's boogie box on the shelf.

M.S.P LYMOL

Big D and Fez (the blonde). The P.T.I. Other names I'm not sure. The top of Billy the Kid's head and bottom right Big H in the audience.

29th June 1982.

Post (I'd actually written *pre*) Sod's Opera. It was enjoyed by all.

The watches will be going back to 1:3 the first leave party go from Ascension in the morning. Reached Ascension and set off at 1600 for Gib. So some got the chance of leaving early to go home from Ascension by plane.

Not a choice I'd have made as we were going to Gibraltar for a run ashore before going home to Rosyth. We were begging to go into Lisbon for a quick run ashore too but that fell on deaf ears.

30th June 1982.

Did a figure of 8 knot in the equator at 2025.

Steve's comment "won't it be dragged with us now?"

1st July 1982.

Crossing the line ceremony at the Court of King Neptune on the flight deck.

The lads rigged up a pool from plastic sheeting and filled it with water and attached a gang plank. The ceremony involved certain members of the ships company having to walk the plank. I think if I remember right, the pool was full of bubbles too.

At around about this time I took my turn on the satellite radio telephone. I rang home... The first time obviously that I'd spoken to Mum and Dad since before we left for Gib. They said that they'd been told to expect bad news because the Argentinians had reported HMS Plymouth as sunk! No known survivors! I don't think they'd given up on me, but it must have been one almighty relief that we were ok! They literally didn't know for over two weeks if I was dead or alive...

2nd July 1982.

Hands to bathe, good fun!

Oh I remember this day! We were well away from the shark infested water of Ascension. Even though, the Sea Rider was deployed with a couple of lads armed with SLR rifles, just in case. This wasn't the first time I'd had a chance to have a wash, I'd taken that opportunity as soon as I could after the surrender, and so did everyone else I think. It really is quite amazing just how smelly you get if you don't wash. Although I think I've probably met a few individuals since, who stink even more than I did!

As soon as the OOW made the announcement that we were going to hands to bathe, the ship came to a stop in the water and everyone rushed around to get their swimming gear on. Some just jumped overboard. A rope net was dropped over the side to clamber back on board by. I went down below and got my trunks on (yes it was normal once to wear budgie smugglers). I went up to the bridge and out of the bridge door. I looked over (where the Loan Bean had been months before) and I could see the Sea Rider and most of the crew, splashing about down there in the water, diving off the side and having a great time. I climbed up onto the duckboards and stood on the edge of the bridge wing, holding onto the 10" lantern for balance... I steadied myself with my toes gripping the beading, bent the knees and dived from the highest point I've ever dived from before - or since. Probably over thirty feet to the water and BAM! I smashed into the water. It was two miles deep, I'd gone in quite cleanly and the water was really warm, I just wanted to stay in that position going through the water with the momentum from the dive. I slowed up, it felt like I was quite deep, I looked back, in the clear water and I could see the huge hull of the ship just floating there, beyond the bottom of the hull it was darkness. I must have been there for a couple of seconds taking it all in, then I thought of a fucking great Hammer Head coming gracefully towards me (a mere snack). So I let myself float sharpish to the surface, I swam back to the net and clambered out. We had a while there, dive bombing off the flight deck and messing about, it was brilliant!

3rd July 1982.

HMS Rhyl, Danae and Diomede are creeping up on us for a pretend attack 12deg 42'North 17' 52.5w 350 @14.

5th July 1982.

Passing the islands of Fuerteventura and Lanzarote in Islas Canarias. I've heard it's a nice place! We were too far away to see much. Horse racing on the flight deck. Betting with model horses, an excuse for more beer really.

England out of the World Cup!

7th July 1982. Day 101.

Entering Gib, a nice sight. A fantastic welcome with a large crowd, ships hooters going etc.

Land at last after 101 days at sea!

The Chiefs were all dressed as Uncle Alberts, complete with chinless beards and walking sticks, waving them at the huge crowd on the quayside and crammed onto balconies. The Gibraltar Guard was there, I recognised a mate who I knew called Moss in the parade and he was stood to attention with an SLR at his side. I hoisted the Jack when that rope went over the bollard. The weather was beautiful, apparently Steve Walters was there too! We got ready pretty quickly for the run ashore that evening, I can tell you! No scrutinising at the gangway for that run ashore!

I have no further memory of that day at all!

9th July 1982.

What happened to the 8th?

Departing Gibraltar with an even bigger crowd, a band, parade, hangovers etc. and a departure to remember. (It's a bit of a blur still if I'm honest!)

What's Rosyth going to be like? Slow passage back very boring but it's not long now. The days are dragging!! And the weather isn't quite so tropical.

This was when I had the idea to write down all the notes I had made in the Bridge Tactical Log, just in case I might want to recall my experiences one day. I wished now that I'd written more. I also wish I'd taken more photographs!

11th July 1982.

Slowly getting closer, just at the bottom of the Bay of Biscay.

12th July 1982.

(Little bit from Knotty)

We're just off the Coast of Plymouth, it's rough and bucketing down with rain (did we honestly want to come home to sunny old England?)

0645 morning watch bye bye.

Tommy Doak threw the log over the side. My bobble hat suffered the same fate.

14th July 1982.

LAST DAY.

The day we got into Rosyth. There was a huge crowd waiting for us, people on the bridges with banners and the dock yard was packed with people, waving and *cheering.* THAT was an understatement…

I was dressed, as was everyone else, in my No1's and as we entered the Firth of Forth. The whole ships Co. all on the upper deck dressed immaculately in No1's, I made my way with the Union Jack, stuffed into its bag, to the very front of the ship, hooked the top and bottom Inglefield clips to the Jack Stay line, slid the sliders into the channel going up the staff and tied the bag to the Jack Stay. Once that was set ready to be hoisted, I stood there to take it all in. There were boats gathering and following us in, people on the boats waving and cheering. Tug boats squirting water from high pressure hoses high into the air. As we approached the red masterpiece, I could see that there were people up there with flags, a train had stopped up there, people waving out of the windows, and it was amazing. The huge suspension bridge was the same, traffic stopped and people waving, dropping confetti and cheering as we passed underneath, it was unbelievable! Over to the right another mile or so away, I could see that the shore was lined with people, the dock yard came into view and that was absolutely rammed with people, there was a Royal Marines band, they started to play as we got closer. Hundreds of family members were there on the quayside, everyone cheering us on this old rusty and battle-weary warship with holes still visible in the funnel and patches on the port side. I had the best view in the house, right at the front, balls settling into their usual position (it was warm), I scanned the crowd. I knew Mum & Dad would be in there somewhere, I couldn't see them though. The first line went over the bollard and I hoisted the Jack proudly, Hutch standing right behind me, we came along side. We all 'fell out' and I walked down the port side, there they were! (They'd completely missed me), I ran down to the gangway that was being lowered into place, they all waited patiently till it was secure, then like a human funnel the crowd squeezed down the gangway and the families poured off onto the flight deck and my Mum & Dad spilled out with the rest of them! It was so good to see them. I took them down to the mess, it was absolutely full, standing room only, and we offered out our meagre beer rations and talked and talked. That night, with my parents, Knotty and his (now late) parents and Spider, whose parents didn't attend, went to an Italian restaurant, for good food, big cigars and lots of red wine! I can still remember some of that night strangely, I remember us leaving an empty bottle of wine each at the end of the gangway and thinking the milkman will pick them up in the morning.

Phot; Al McIntyre

We had a couple of hours sleep and we were up for call to hands at early o'clock. I was absolutely hanging! I made my way up to the bridge, we had to go to de-ammunition, further up the river, oh my head! Knotty was with me and Tommy was there. Tommy seemed fine and in control of his actions. Knotty was a slitty eyed mess as was I! I think we were there for about half an hour, we must have been still drunk, breathing fumes and slurring our words because Tommy just said to both of us "fuck off down below before the Captain comes!"

Mum and Dad stayed in a hotel locally and when we came back all sobered up and empty of ammunition, we were allowed home on leave.

My Dad had borrowed an Opel Monza 3.0 from a friend as his TR7 was too small and Mum's car was too old for the long journey home. If I remember rightly, Knotty's parents, Jack & Cis went back home to Bucks on a coach, Knotty came with us. We drove into Mum & Dad's road, their house is at the bottom of the cul-de-sac, the garage at right-angles to the house on the right. A Union Jack covered the sloping roof of the garage facing us as we approached and there was a banner with the words "WELCOME HOME SIMON & KNOTTY!" spread across the double garage door.

My brothers and friends were there, my Gran was there too, and that's when the party started...

Since '82...

A lot has happened, I'm glad to say that I'm part of the ex-crew of HMSP and we enjoy reunions with ex-crew members, the majority from the first commission in 1961. We, The Crew of '82, are the sprogs!

Sadly, on the 20th August 2014, HMSP was unceremoniously towed from her berth in Birkenhead, where she had been left to rot for the last six years. We had been unable to save her from the scrap man. I won't go into the politics of what has happened, it's not for me to say, it's just unfortunate really and very sad that she couldn't have been saved as a museum for generations to take in what it must have been like going to perhaps the last conventional war. HMSP was perfectly preserved inside, my bunk light has stopped working but everything else is as it was. So now as I write, she's a couple of days off the Turkish coastline, there's a rumour that one of the prop shaft seals is leaking and with a bit of luck she'll sink before the Turks get their oxy acetylene torches to her and recycle her without a thought, how would they know?

Around the late eighties, I learned that Jack committed suicide, probably 'post-traumatic stress syndrome' or something. I'd never seen him since, it was so difficult to get in touch with lost friends in those days. But we've gathered a motley crew together since then and enjoy re-cycling our stories over a few beers every year.

It's mad to think that thirty two years have gone by since then, I'm approaching the end of my career in the Plod, my daughter Jenna and my S.I.L. Kevin have produced Little Molly and even littler, Sophie. My son Sam is making his way in business and living the dream in hotter climes. Mrs Riley and I have just celebrated our Silver

Wedding Anniversary and life is pretty good!

At one of our reunions that we usually hold in Liverpool, a few years ago, we had just had a tour around the ship by torchlight and we went to the local pub for a D.T.S. (Dinner Time Session). Someone said to me "hey Spike, there's someone over there wants to speak to you..." It was JACK FUCKING WARNER...

Jack's not in this photo, he got so pissed
the night before – he missed the photo.

So here he is…

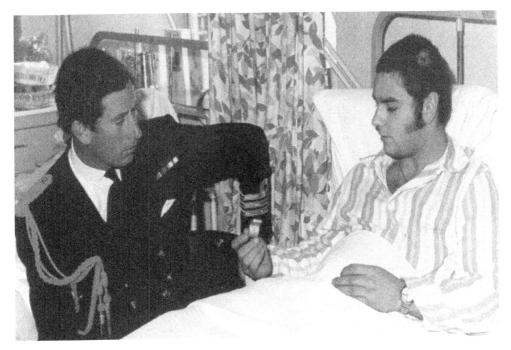

Phot; c/o Jack Warner

Here are some of my cartoons from the time, one is from 1984, when I was on the Glamourous Organ and things hadn't changed. You can also see that I drew them in the dark, or at least with red light, so I couldn't tell if I was drawing in black or blue, you can also see that they were drawn on the back of a message form.

Ah! And you're rapidly becoming a useful member of the team now! are you?
EH?
SPIKE

All photos taken by me or Al McIntyre.

Printed in Great Britain
by Amazon